QUICK & EASY
Salads & Breads with Style

Edie Hand • Darlene Real • Debra Lustrea

Nomad Press
A division of Nomad Communications
10 9 8 7 6 5 4 3 2 1
Copyright © 2003 Nomad Communications and the Edie Hand Foundation
All rights reserved.

No part of this book may be reproduced in any form without permission in writing from the publisher, except by a reviewer who may quote brief passages in a review. The trademark "Nomad Press" and the Nomad Press logo are trademarks of Nomad Communications, Inc. Printed in Canada.

ISBN 0-9722026-2-5

Questions regarding the ordering of this book for the trade should be addressed to:
Independent Publishers Group
814 N. Franklin St.
Chicago, IL 60610
or for individuals go to: www.nomadpress.net

Nomad Press, PO Box 875, Norwich, VT 05055

Dedications

Food, Family & Friends is dedicated to our families . . .

To my son, Linc Hand; my beloved husband, Mark Aldridge; my mother, Sue Blackburn-Hardesty; my dad, Guy Blackburn; and my sister, Kim Poss.
—*Edie Hand*

Thank you to my children, Tracy D. Webber, Rachel Real Poovey, and Richard H. Real III; my mother, LaVerta Firestone-Hartley; and my sister, Debby Reisner-Rose.

—*Darlene Real*

I want to give a special thanks to my children, Tom, Alanna, and Adam, and my dear mom and dad, Eleanor and Frank.

—*Debra Lustrea*

And dedicated to our wonderful friends who support and have contributed to the *Food, Family & Friends* series.

Acknowledgments

I'd like to thank my true friends, Darlene Real and Debra Lustrea, for sharing their talents and knowledge to embark upon the *Food, Family & Friends* series . . . We're a real team!

A special thank you to my husband, Mark Aldridge, and Katie Wilson, my assistant, for extra editing efforts. Thanks also to Fannie Flagg— such a dear friend. My appreciation to Melissa Donaldson, RD, LD with Heart College at HealthSouth; Debbie Francis with Cox Radio Special Events in Jacksonville, FL; Chef Robert of Winn-Dixie in Jacksonville, FL; and to Chef Susan Notter and Ken Horn of Culinard Institute of Virginia College. Additionally, thanks to David Bell with Moore's Marinade; Dana Emery of Unilever/Bestfoods; Richard Epstein, associated with Camp Seale Harris for Juvenile diabetes camps; and the Diabetes Trust Fund, etc.

I owe tremendous gratitude to Alex Kahan for believing in the project and Darlene, Debra, and myself . . . and additional thanks to Lauri, Susan, and Rachel—and Nomad Press's entire staff; you all are the best!

—Edie Hand

A portion of the proceeds from *Food, Family & Friends* will go to the Edie Hand Foundation, which will benefit the American Diabetes Association and juvenile diabetic camps across the region.

Edie uses **Jenn-Air/Maytag** products and **Demarle** gourmet tools at home and on tour.

A special thanks to Wyndham Hotels and American Airlines for making the *Food, Family & Friends* tour with the Southern Women's Shows and Cox Radio's Special Events even more a reality.

Visit www.ediehandfoundation.org and click on Books for more information about the *Food, Family & Friends* tours or visit www.southernshows.com. Also please see www.jennair.com, www.maytag.com and www.gourmettools.com

Table of Contents

Salads

Ambrosia	2
Artichoke Feta Cheese Salad	4
Avocado Grapefruit Salad	6
California Chicken Salad	8
Chicken-Nectarine-Apple Salad	10
Chinese Chicken Salad	12
Concert in the Park Chicken Salad	14
Crown Chicken Salad	16
Crunchy Pea Salad	18
Curried Couscous	20
Dilly of a Potato Salad	22
Fettuccine Salad	24
Fix it Fast and Forget it Slaw	26
Fruit Compote	28

Garden Current Salad	30
Green Bean Salad and New Potatoes	32
Heavenly Coleslaw	34
Italian Pasta and Vegetable Salad	36
Layered Sunburst Salad	38
Marinated Salad	42
Min-tee Melon Salad	44
New Potato Salad	46
Panzanella	48
Peary Salad	50
Shrimp Pasta Vegetable Salad	52
Shrimp Salad	54
Simply Special Wild Rice Salad	56
Spinach Berry Salad	58
Taco Chicken Salad	60
Tenderloin Summer Salad	62

Tuna Bean Salad 64
Turkey Spring Greens 66

Dressings

American, French, Greek, Vinaigrette.. 68
Italian, Oriental, Polynesian, Swiss, African, Spanish Vinaigrette 69
Buttermilk Salad Dressing.. 70
Dijon Vinaigrette Dressing 70
Honey Mustard Salad Dressing 71

Breads

Applesauce Coffee Bread... 74
Banana Nut Bread 76
Banana Oatmeal Bread 77
Basic White Bread 78
Date Bread 79

Diabetic Cheddar Cornbread	80
Dilly Bread	81
Fiesta Corn Sticks	82
French Bread	83
Grandmother's Cranberry Bread	85
Lemon Bread	86
Milk Buscuits	87
Onion Dill Bread	88
Peach Tea Bread	89
Peanut Butter Bread	91
Pumpkin Surprise Bread	92
Quick and Easy Coffee Cake	93
Quick Potato Bread	94
Savory Orange Bread	95
Scratch Biscuits	96

Special Strawberry Bread	97
Spicy Cheese Straws	98
Whole Wheat Bread	100
Helpful Hints for Baking Bread	101

Etiquette and Style

Place Setting	104
Napkins	105
The Basics of Dining Etiquette	106
The Right Attitude with Real Manners	109

Know Your Ingredients

Conversion Tables	112
Recipe Modifications/Substitutions	114
Exchanges and Nutrition Tips	116

Dear Friends,

Over 15 million Americans are affected by Type 2 diabetes. This number will increase dramatically in the future without a change in eating habits and an increase in regular physical activity. Reports released by the C.D.C. in June 2003 predict that one in three children born on or after 2000 will develop diabetes because of their diet and lack of regular exercise. Today Type 2 diabetes, which is also called "adult onset diabetes," is being diagnosed in young people.

So many of us live with diabetes, or know someone — friend, family member, or colleague — who has the disease. Both of my grandmothers, two nieces, and a nephew live with, or have lived with, the complications of some form of diabetes for many years. I am pleased to help raise awareness of the importance of eating healthier through the *Food, Family & Friends* cookbook series.

You'll find some of my favorite recipes in this cookbook. Debra Lustrea and I have offered our treasured family recipes, with adaptations to make them more diabetic friendly. A few come from an earlier book of mine, *Recipes for Life*, also with diabetic adaptations in mind. Enjoy—and remember to exercise, eat right, and get lots of rest. We are all in this together.

—Edie Hand

Note: Consult with your physician or your local Diabetes Association Chapter for a healthy lifestyle plan.

Diabetes contact information:
American Diabetes Association: www.diabetes.org or 800-DIABETES
American Dietetic Association: Nutritional information hotline at 800-366-1655
Diabetes Trust Fund: Research information at www.diabetestrustfund.org or 800-577-1383
Juvenile Diabetes: www.childrenwithdiabetes.com

Salads

Ambrosia

1 cup white grapes, cut in half
1 cup canned mandarin oranges, well-drained
1 cup canned pineapple chunks, well-drained
1 cup sliced bananas
1 cup coconut flakes
1 cup mini marshmallows
1 cup vanilla yogurt
1 cup halved pecans

Mix all ingredients except nuts together in a large bowl. Cover and chill overnight in the refrigerator.

Serve on a large lettuce leaf or get really creative and serve in a half section of coconut shell, or in a half-cut scooped pineapple or watermelon bowl. For added flavor add one teaspoon orange juice or coconut milk. Garnish each serving with nuts. Serves 4.

FOOD EXCHANGES: Carbohydrate: 3; Protein: 1; Fat: 4
BREAD SUGGESTION: Banana Nut Bread

REAL STYLE
Presentation Supplies:
- *Wide mouth vase or clear cylinder 8 to 10 inches tall*
- *Dry white rice to fill vase three-fourths full*
- *Three to five white, tapered candles*
- *Ribbon/raffia*
- *Pale yellow or white napkins*

Create an elegant centerpiece with three to five white taper candles placed in a wide mouth vase filled with rice. You can buy inexpensive cylinder vases at your local discount store. Place the candles in the rice at an angle so that about ⅓ of candle is in the rice. Tie an orange, yellow, green, or white ribbon, loop of raffia, or napkin around the base of the cylinder to provide a colorful accent.

For a beautiful salad presentation, place the chilled ingredients in one half of a trimmed, flat bottomed, scooped pineapple or melon for individual servings. Place each half on a breakfast plate with an orange slice and cherry on the left-hand side of the plate for garnish, leaving the right side of the plate for bread. Add maraschino cherries, walnuts, or pecans to garnish the top of the salad.

Artichoke Feta Cheese Salad

- ⅓ cup olive oil
- ½ cup red wine vinegar
- 1½ teaspoons salt
- 1 teaspoon sugar
- ¼ teaspoon pepper
- 1 large head romaine or bib lettuce
- 1 can artichoke hearts, drained and cut in half
- ¾ cup crumbled feta cheese

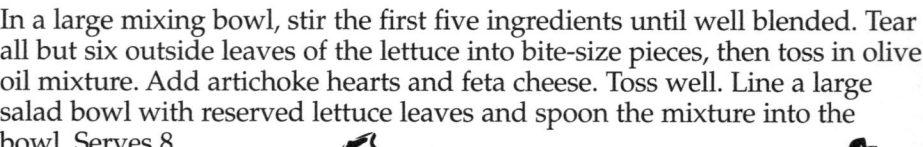

In a large mixing bowl, stir the first five ingredients until well blended. Tear all but six outside leaves of the lettuce into bite-size pieces, then toss in olive oil mixture. Add artichoke hearts and feta cheese. Toss well. Line a large salad bowl with reserved lettuce leaves and spoon the mixture into the bowl. Serves 8.

FOOD EXCHANGES: Carbohydrate: 0; Protein: 0; Fat: 2
BREAD SUGGESTION: Basic White Bread

REAL STYLE
Presentation Supplies:
- Clear individual salad bowls or one large salad bowl
- One medium-size, clear bowl for centerpiece
- Three to five flowers or floating candles
- White napkins and napkin rings/ribbon

Bring sparkle and clean lines to your dining table with cut crystal or pressed glass bowls. Start your collection of glassware in all shapes and sizes—check out antique, discount, and craft stores for the best buys. You may be one of those blessed folks who already has heirlooms from generations past.

For an easy and elegant centerpiece, use a medium-size, shallow, clear bowl filled three-quarters full with water. Float three or five flowers in the water, or if fresh flowers are unavailable, use white floating candles. Add white paper or fabric napkins held with napkins rings or tied with ribbons. White lends a pure feeling that blends well with glass dishes.

To create a beautiful salad presentation, line the sides of one large salad bowl or several smaller individual bowls with outside, larger lettuce leaves. For a touch of contrast, top the salad with large Spanish olives stuffed with pimentos. Place one on top of each individual serving, or seven to nine on top of a large serving bowl. Scatter carrot shavings made with a potato peeler or grater over top of salad or add one large carrot curl.

Avocado Grapefruit Salad

- 4 avocados
- juice of 1 lemon
- 1 pound cooked crabmeat, flaked
- ½ cup canned pears, drained and diced
- ¾ cup light mayonnaise
- 1 cup grapefruit sections
- 2 teaspoons ketchup
- ½ cup pecans
- several lettuce leaves
- black olives for garnish
- dash of Worcestershire sauce or Moore's Marinade™, to taste

Cut the avocados in half and remove the pit from each. Rub lemon juice on avocado to prevent discoloration. Place both avocado halves on lettuce leaves in salad plates. Combine crabmeat with all other ingredients and fill the avocado cavities. Mixture will overflow to the bed of lettuce.

Garnish each salad with a black olive. Serves 4.

FOOD EXCHANGES: Carbohydrate: 1; Protein: 4; Fat: 4
BREAD SUGGESTION: Fiesta Corn Sticks

REAL STYLE
Presentation Supplies:
- *Three clear bowls*
- *Variety of cut ivy strands or ivy plants*
- *Sand or small polished or plain stones*
- *Three tall, tapered candles*
- *Round or rectangular placemats, yellow napkins*

Match the color of the salad with a centerpiece of combined ivy bowls. Place three clear bowls in the center of the table, and fill each bowl with sand or small stones. Place one tapered candle firmly into the center of the stones in each bowl, then fill each bowl one third full with water and tuck ivy around each candle.

Serve iced tea in tall glasses with rounds of lemons. Fold yellow napkins to left of flatware.

California Chicken Salad

3 cups torn iceberg lettuce
2 cups torn spinach leaves, stems removed
2 cups blackened cooked chicken breast, chopped into bite-sized pieces
2 oranges, peeled and sectioned
1 pink grapefruit, peeled and sectioned
1 ripe avocado, peeled and cubed
1 cup slivered almonds, toasted

In a large bowl, toss together all salad ingredients except for almonds. When you are ready to serve, toss salad again, then top with almonds. Choose a vinaigrette dressing from the selection following the salads section. This may be served family-style in a large bowl or on individual salad plates. Serves 4.

FOOD EXCHANGES: Carbohydrate: 2; Protein: 5; Fat: 1.5
BREAD SUGGESTION: Banana Nut Bread

REAL STYLE
Presentation supplies:
- *Empty wine bottles, small, medium, large*
- *Three tall tapers*
- *Wax crayons and old candles to drip down bottles*
- *Kumquats and unshelled almonds*
- *Woven place mats and white tablecloth*
- *Napkins in either rust, orange, or sage*
- *Wine glasses*

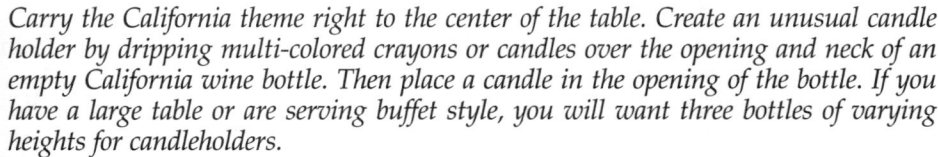

Carry the California theme right to the center of the table. Create an unusual candle holder by dripping multi-colored crayons or candles over the opening and neck of an empty California wine bottle. Then place a candle in the opening of the bottle. If you have a large table or are serving buffet style, you will want three bottles of varying heights for candleholders.

Scatter fresh green or fall leaves around the base of the bottles, and add a handful of colorful kumquats and seven to nine unshelled almonds. Woven placemats extend the earthy theme, but you can also dress up this look with a white tablecloth and place the mats on top of the cloth. Use neutrals, orange, sage, or rust hues for mats and (paper or cloth) napkins to accent the table decor.

Wine and water glasses should be placed to the right side of the table setting, at the top of the knife. Place napkins in the center of each dinner plate until all guests are seated. After your guests have removed their napkins, place a salad plate on each dinner plate.

Chicken-Nectarine-Apple Salad

- 3 cups cubed, cooked chicken
- 3 medium nectarines, pitted and thinly sliced
- 1½ cups peeled, cored, and diced red delicious apples
- 1 tablespoon thinly sliced green onion
- 1 tablespoon thinly sliced celery
- 1 cup toasted, slivered almonds
  fresh nectarine wedges for garnish
  leaf lettuce for garnish

In a large bowl, combine the chicken, nectarines, apples, green onion, and celery. Pour the vinaigrette of your choice (see dressings section after salads) over the chicken mixture, and toss lightly to mix. Cover and chill for several hours in the refrigerator. When you are ready to serve, add the toasted almonds and toss the salad once more. Serve in a lettuce-lined bowl, and top with nectarine wedges. Serves 6.

FOOD EXCHANGES: Carbohydrate: 2; Protein: 4; Fat: 3
BREAD SUGGESTION: Special Strawberry Bread

REAL STYLE
Presentation supplies:
- *Two black wood stands or clay saucers spray painted black and turned upside down*
- *Two pillar candles*
- *Large animal print scarf or unhemmed animal print fabric*
- *Five small clay pots painted black for votive candles*
- *Five votive candles*
- *Black or gold paper or plastic dishes*

Animal prints are the theme for this presentation. Begin with black, gold, cream, or bronze colors. If you have animal print items or small animal figurines in other parts of your home, use them as part of this table setting. Use black stands to display pillar candles, then place the votive candles in the five small clay pots. Use black or gold napkins and plates to complement the colors of the animal prints. Wrap the napkins with grape vines for an unusual napkin ring.

Chinese Chicken Salad

3 cups torn lettuce
1½ cups diagonally cut cooked chicken
¼ cup sliced water chestnuts
½ cup julienned carrots
¼ cup bamboo shoots
½ cup snow pea pods
¼ cup chopped red cabbage
¼ cup diagonally sliced green onions
1 clove garlic, pressed or chopped
chow mein noodles

Dressing

3½ tablespoons soy sauce
2 tablespoons canola oil
2 tablespoons rice vinegar
1 tablespoon sugar
½ teaspoon dried mustard
½ teaspoon garlic powder
½ teaspoon black pepper
½ teaspoon sesame oil

In a large bowl, toss all of the salad ingredients together and chill. To make the dressing, mix all the ingredients together in a medium-sized fruit jar with a lid. Immediately before serving, shake the dressing ingredients to completely mix, pour over the salad, and gently toss. Serve on individual salad plates. Garnish with chow mein noodles. Serves 6.

FOOD EXCHANGES: Carbohydrate: 0; Protein: 3; Fat: 0
BREAD SUGGESTION: Savory Orange Bread

REAL STYLE
Presentation supplies:
- *Red cabbage leaves*
- *Asian artifacts*
- *Two pillar candles*
- *Small bamboo [art or garden supply store]*
- *Hot glue and cording*
- *Black or plum-colored napkins and place mats*

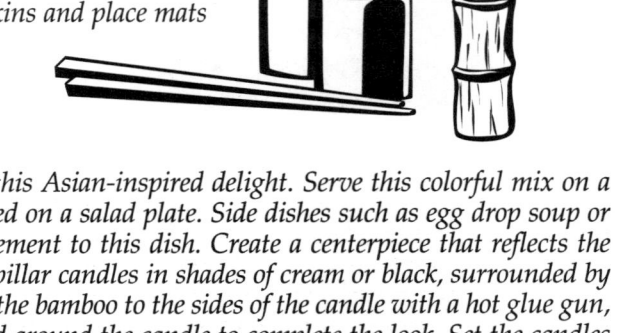

Get out your chopsticks for this Asian-inspired delight. Serve this colorful mix on a large leaf of red cabbage placed on a salad plate. Side dishes such as egg drop soup or wontons are a perfect complement to this dish. Create a centerpiece that reflects the Asian theme with two large pillar candles in shades of cream or black, surrounded by odd lengths of bamboo. Glue the bamboo to the sides of the candle with a hot glue gun, then tie a length of black cord around the candle to complete the look. Set the candles in the center of table, and add any Asian-themed artifacts you may own.

Use napkins and placemats that match the color of the candles. Serve hot teas during the beginning of the evening, when guests arrive, or at the end of the meal. Add to the ambiance of aromas with green, jasmine, or herbal teas.

Concert in the Park Chicken Salad

- 1 head lettuce, torn into bits
- 2 pounds cooked chicken breast, shredded
- 2 large tomatoes, diced
- 1 avocado, diced
- ½ pound cooked turkey bacon, crumbled

Dressing

- ½ cup oil
- 2 teaspoons sugar
- 1 teaspoon salt
- ⅓ cup minced parsley
- ¼ cup white wine vinegar
- ½ teaspoon black pepper
- 1¾ teaspoons dry mustard
- 1 clove garlic, minced

In a large mixing bowl layer salad ingredients, beginning with the lettuce, followed by chicken breast, tomatoes, avocado, and bacon. Combine dressing ingredients in a small bowl and pour over salad. Toss and serve immediately into individual bowls. Serves 6.

FOOD EXCHANGES: Carbohydrate: 1; Protein: 4; Fat: 9
BREAD SUGGESTION: Banana Oatmeal Bread

REAL STYLE

Presentation supplies:

- Clear wine glasses
- Tall cylinder
- Black paint
- Pencil erasers
- Rock salt for cylinder
- Three to five black taper candles
- White napkins, plates, and bowls
- White coffee filters

Recreate the ambiance of a musical evening showered with candlelight. Black and white is the theme for this luncheon or dinner salad. The day before your get-together, create a terrific centerpiece by painting a clear cylinder with black polka dots using a pencil eraser dipped in black paint as your brush. Carry the black-and-white polka dot theme through to wine or water glasses by painting them the same way. Purchase black and white polka dot fabric to cut for napkins, or purchase black paper napkins and tie them with a white ribbon. On the day of the party, fill the painted cylinder with rock salt and place three black tapers in it. Use a white tablecloth and serving dishes that compliment this table. **Serve the salad in a soup bowl** *placed on top of a white doily or coffee liner, and top the salad with fresh parsley. Play soothing music to complete the mood.*

Crown Chicken Salad

- 4 cups cubed, cooked chicken
- 1 cup chopped celery
- ½ cup chopped yellow peppers
- ½ cup chopped green onions
- 2 tablespoons chopped pimento
- ½ cup whole cashews
- 6 medium tomatoes cut in half with a crown cutter

Ranch Dressing

- 1 cup low-fat buttermilk
- ½ cup medium salsa
- 3 tablespoons low-fat mayonnaise
- 2 tablespoons chopped fresh parsley
- 1 tablespoon lemon juice
- ½ teaspoon sugar
- ½ teaspoon dry mustard
- ¼ teaspoon salt
- ¼ teaspoon pepper
- 1 clove garlic, chopped

(Note that this dressing can be safely stored in the refrigerator for up to two weeks.)

Combine all dressing ingredients in a blender until smooth. Place in an airtight jar and chill. Mix the first five salad ingredients together in a large bowl. Combine the dressing from the jar and toss lightly. Mix in cashews before serving in tomato halves on salad plates. Serves 6.

FOOD EXCHANGES: Carbohydrate: 0; Protein: 5.5; Fat: 0
BREAD SUGGESTION: Spicy Cheese Straws

REAL STYLE
Presentation supplies:
- *Red, white, and blue bow*
- *White paper or plastic dishes*
- *White napkins*
- *Angel food cake, strawberries*
- *Flag toothpicks*

Combine business with patriotism and good food. Invite your office in or take a special lunch to your clients. Have the power lunch in the boardroom or in your corporate dining room. Place a red, white, and blue bow on the office door or at the front desk to welcome colleagues. No centerpiece will be needed for this event.

Give your guests a treat with this new twist on traditional chicken salad. Place the cored tomatoes on leafy pieces of radicchio lettuce and fill the tomatoes with chicken salad. Garnish the tops with a touch of mayonnaise, then top them with a pimento and a dash of paprika. Place small toothpick flags in the pimento.

Provide a variety of crackers, breads, and cheeses, as well as coffee, tea, and water with lemon or soft drinks. Include a slice of angel food cake with strawberries for a sweet ending.

Crunchy Pea Salad

- 1 cup diced celery
- 1 cup chopped cauliflower
- 1 10-ounce package frozen peas
- 1 cup cashews
- ½ cup light sour cream or plain yogurt
- 1 tablespoon dill
- 1 slice bacon, cooked and crumbled for garnish

Combine first six ingredients in a large bowl and chill. Immediately before serving, garnish with crumbled bacon and place in individual salad bowls. Serves 4.

FOOD EXCHANGES: Carbohydrate: 1.5; Protein: 1; Fat: 4
BREAD SUGGESTION: Whole Wheat Bread

REAL STYLE
Presentation supplies:
- Yellow and white poster board, butcher paper, or construction paper
- Clear or bright colored vase
- Fresh or paper flowers
- Yellow, green, or white napkins
- White or yellow string, twine, or ribbon

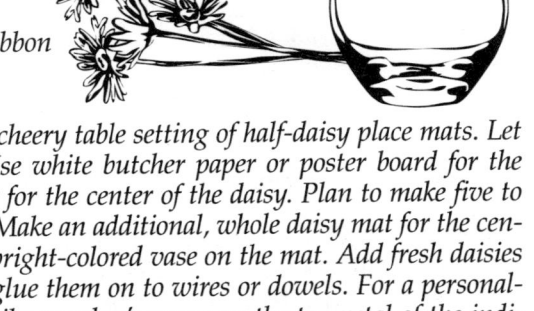

Children and adults alike will love a cheery table setting of half-daisy place mats. Let the children help create the mats. Use white butcher paper or poster board for the petals and yellow construction paper for the center of the daisy. Plan to make five to seven petals and a half-moon center. Make an additional, whole daisy mat for the center of the table, then place a clear or bright-colored vase on the mat. Add fresh daisies to the vase or create paper ones and glue them on to wires or dowels. For a personalized touch, write each guest's or family member's name on the top petal of the individual daisy place mats. Draw eyes and a happy mouth on the center of all mats; when the plates are removed, your guests will still be smiling. To complete the look, use yellow, green or white napkins, tied with raffia.

For a terrific salad presentation, place romaine lettuce leaves on individual salad plates. Fill each leaf with salad and garnish with cooked, chopped bacon and small cubes of mild red and yellow peppers. Serve your favorite wheat bread from a napkin-lined basket. Remember to provide bread and butter plates for guests.

Curried Couscous

- 2 tablespoons butter
- 3 cups diced fresh vegetables, such as bell peppers, broccoli florets, cauliflower florets, julienned carrots, and red onion
- 1½ teaspoons curry powder
- ⅛ teaspoon cayenne pepper
- ¼ cup dried cranberries
- 1 cup couscous, uncooked
- 2 cups cooked turkey or ham, cut into strips
- 1 can (14 ounce) vegetable broth

Melt the butter in a large saucepan over medium heat. Add vegetables and saute until tender. Add the curry powder, cayenne pepper, and cranberries, and simmer. Add the couscous and meat, then cover, turn off heat, and let stand for five minutes or until the liquid is absorbed. Place the couscous mixture in a large serving bowl, fluff with a fork and cool before serving buffet style. Serve with toppings as desired, such as chopped apples, toasted almonds, chopped cilantro, and plain yogurt. Serves 4.

FOOD EXCHANGES: Carbohydrate: 2.5; Protein: 5; Fat: 1
BREAD SUGGESTION: Date Bread

REAL STYLE
Presentation supplies:
- *Coral or navy napkins*
- *Painted pottery or stoneware dishes*
- *Wrought iron or wooden candlesticks*
- *Five to seven candles*
- *Watering can, fresh or silk geraniums*

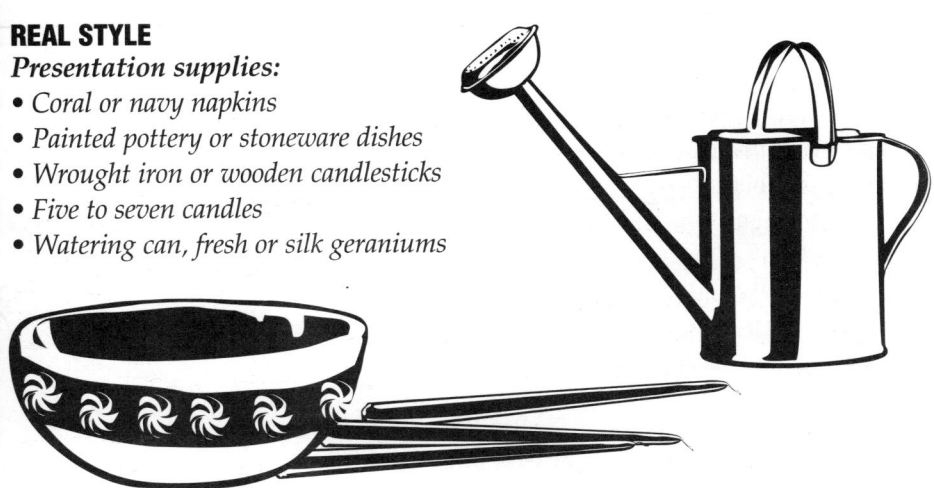

This is a marvelous Moroccan dish. Serve this dish buffet style, and offer the many suggested toppings in multi-colored painted pottery bowls or plates. Cloth napkins and flatware can be rolled together, which will be easy for guests to pick up as they begin their buffet. Dress the table with wrought-iron or wooden candlesticks, or place the candles in clear, tall glasses. Use festive orange or coral-colored napkins. A watering can filled with fresh or silk geraniums adds a finishing touch.

Dilly of a Potato Salad

- **4** large, unpeeled Idaho potatoes, cooked and cut in thin slices.
- **1** large white onion cut in very thin slices
- **1** cup low-fat mayonnaise
- **⅓** cup lemon juice
- **1** teaspoon sugar
- **1** teaspoon dill
- **1** teaspoon dill seed
- **½** teaspoon salt
- **1** tablespoon white vinegar

Place potatoes and onions in a large mixing bowl. Mix remaining ingredients in another large bowl. Taste and adjust to your own liking. Using a ladle, pour the dressing mixture over the sliced potatoes and onions. Mix thoroughly and chill for 30 minutes. Serve on salad plates or heavy plastic plates if you're on a picnic. Serves 8.

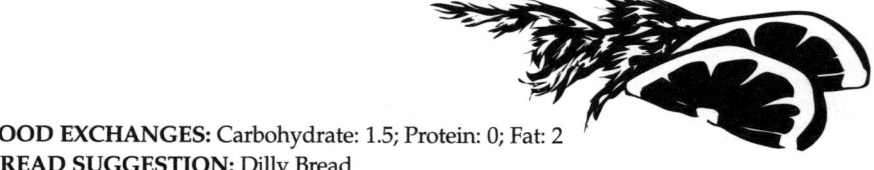

FOOD EXCHANGES: Carbohydrate: 1.5; Protein: 0; Fat: 2
BREAD SUGGESTION: Dilly Bread

REAL STYLE

Presentation supplies:

- *Checked tablecloth in shades of red and white or blue and white*
- *Checked napkins*
- *Red or blue small paper or plastic plates*
- *Pitcher*
- *Small white doilies*
- *Green or variegated ivy*

You are ready for a cookout with this old-world salad. Chilled and garnished with parsley, this tasty dish is a great addition to a barbeque or a Sunday picnic. Use traditional red and white, or blue and white checked tablecloth, napkins, and other accessories for your table and use any old or new pitcher filled with green or variegated ivy for your centerpiece. Place individual servings of your dilly potatoes on a white doily on a small colored plate.

Fettuccine Salad

- 6 ounces uncooked fettuccine, broken in half
- 2½ cups broccoli florets
- 1 cup diagonally sliced carrots
- ¾ cup diagonally sliced celery
- ⅓ cup fat-free Italian dressing
- ⅓ cup low-fat mayonnaise
- 2½ teaspoons prepared horseradish
- ½ teaspoon freshly ground pepper
- 12 cherry tomatoes, halved

Cook fettuccine according to package directions. Drain and rinse under cold water. Drain again and set aside.

Cook broccoli, carrots, and celery in a small amount of boiling water for six minutes or until crisp-tender. Drain; plunge into ice water, and drain again.

Combine the cooked fettuccine and vegetables in a large bowl. Combine Italian dressing, mayonnaise, horseradish, and pepper. Stir well and add to the fettuccine mixture. Toss gently. Stir in tomatoes. Serve in large individual pasta bowls and place a plate underneath each bowl. Serves 8.

FOOD EXCHANGES: Carbohydrate: 2; Protein: 2; Fat: 1
BREAD SUGGESTION: Onion Dill Bread

REAL STYLE
Presentation supplies:
- *Individual, white pasta or salad bowls*
- *Quilt or bedspread in pastel colors*
- *Soup tureen*
- *Fresh flowers*
- *Pasta spoons [large kitchen spoons]*
- *Hand-made corsage from ribbon, rattle and diaper pins*

Choose a color scheme for this Italian salad that coordinates with a celebration for a baby shower. Large white pasta bowls placed on dinner plates are the perfect dinnerware for serving this dish. Use either a pastel quilt or a white chenille bedspread for a tablecloth if the gender of the baby is not known. When the gender is established use accessories in blue or pink, including matching napkins. For a playful centerpiece, fill a soup tureen with blue hydrangeas for boys and pink roses for girls, or consider yellow daisies. Garnish the salad with sliced almonds and provide a pasta spoon for eating this dish.

Make a corsage for the guest of honor. Purchase a rattle or flat shaker, tie ribbon with a triple bow around the rattle, add baby's breath or carnation if desired. Place one or three diaper pins on the bow.

Fix it Fast and Forget it Slaw

9 cups shredded white cabbage
3 cups shredded red cabbage
1 large red onion, chopped
1 yellow bell pepper, chopped
2 carrots, peeled and shredded
1 head celery stalks, chopped
1 cup sugar

Dressing

1 teaspoon dry mustard
1 teaspoon celery seeds
1 teaspoon salt
1 teaspoon pepper
2 teaspoons sugar
1 cup white vinegar
¾ cup canola oil

Toss together all the slaw ingredients and the sugar in a large mixing bowl. Set aside. Mix together the dressing ingredients in a medium mixing bowl and pour over the cabbage mixture. Chill covered, in the refrigerator, for 24 hours before serving. Serves 20+.

FOOD EXCHANGES: Carbohydrate: 1; Protein: 0; Fat: 1.5
BREAD SUGGESTION: Spicy Cheese Straws

REAL STYLE

Presentation supplies:

- *Seven to ten clay pots, and saucers varying in sizes*
- *Clay saucers for serving pieces*
- *Red-and-white-checked dish towels or fabric*
- *Red-and-white-checked napkins*
- *Three pillar candles*
- *Three votive candles*
- *Fresh geraniums, daisies, or ivy*

This table presentation is ideal for an indoor or outdoor buffet table. Place a large pot lined with checked fabric in the center of the dining or buffet table. Place a plastic pot of geraniums or daises inside the pot. Add two medium-sized clay pots to the table, one lined with checked fabric for silverware, the other unlined for rolled, vertical-standing napkins. Then place three medium pots for pillar candles and three mini pots for votive candles. Use a mini pot lined with wax paper for toothpicks for hors d'oeuvres or fruit. Use varying sizes of clay saucers as serving platters for bread, bar-b-que, corn-on-the-cob, potato salad, fruits, and desserts. Line each saucer with wax paper before placing foods.

Etiquette hint: *Create cards detailing the menu and place the cards at either end of your buffet table. You can also display the recipes and invitation on the table, as well, if you wish.*

Fruit Compote

1 cup peeled, cored and diced fresh pineapple
1 cup peeled and cubed papaya
1 cup peeled and cubed mango
1 cup peeled and sliced banana
1 cup peeled and sliced apples
1 cup peeled and sliced peaches
1 cup peeled and sliced pears
Apples and pears should be tossed
with lemon juice to prevent discolorization

Dressing
3 tablespoons orange juice
2 tablespoons lime juice
2 tablespoons honey
1 tablespoon freshly grated ginger root
1 stick of cinnamon

Prepare all of the above fruits. These can be prepared ahead of time and stored in air-tight plastic bags or containers. Mix together all of the fruit and let sit for one hour.

Combine the dressing ingredients in a glass microwaveable bowl, and bring to a quick boil in the microwave. Cool for at least one hour, then pour over the fruit mixture before serving in individual bowls.

FOOD EXCHANGES: Carbohydrate: 1.5; Protein: 0; Fat: 0
BREAD SUGGESTION: Lemon Bread

If you prefer, you can mix in either two tablespoons tequila, sake, rum, wine, or brandy to the dressing ingredients. Your choice can be dictated by theme, the other foods you are serving, and if you are serving this as a side salad, as a main dish with bread and cheese, or as a dessert. Your choice will determine the china used. Serves 8.

REAL STYLE
Presentation supplies:
- *Fresh flowers or narcissus bulbs*
- *Deep, clear bowl for forcing bulbs*
- *Compote dishes*
- *Three votive candles*
- *White napkins*

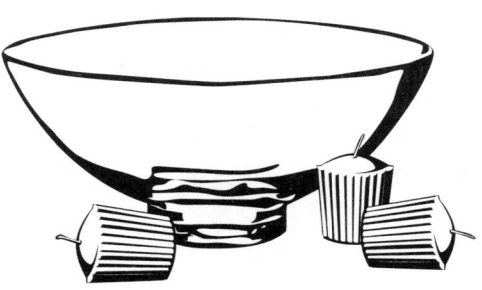

Bring a breath of spring to a winter's table by creating a centerpiece that features forced paper white or narcissus bulbs. Plant one to three bulbs in a deep, clear bowl in early winter or purchase the blooming plants in the supermarket floral department or florist. For warmer months, or when blooming bulbs are not available, use fresh roses, daisies, golden rod, or Queen Anne's lace. Accent the flowering centerpiece with three compote dishes holding votive candles. Place the candles around the centerpiece. Use white napkins to complement the flowering bulbs.

Garden Current Salad

- **1 cup low-fat mayonnaise**
- **¼ cup sugar**
- **3 tablespoons lemon juice**
- **3 cups broccoli florets, steamed 5–8 minutes and cooled**
- **3 cup cauliflower florets, steamed 5–8 minutes and cooled**
- **1 cup thinly sliced red onion**
- **1 cup peeled, shredded carrots**
- **½ cup dried cranberries**
- **½ cup golden raisins**

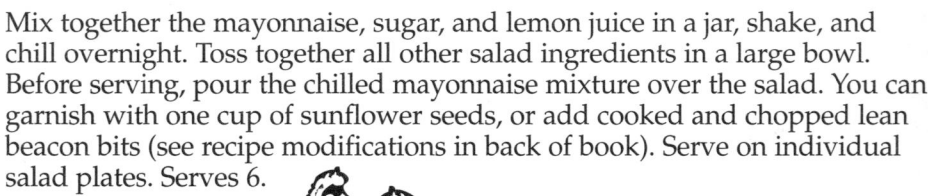

Mix together the mayonnaise, sugar, and lemon juice in a jar, shake, and chill overnight. Toss together all other salad ingredients in a large bowl. Before serving, pour the chilled mayonnaise mixture over the salad. You can garnish with one cup of sunflower seeds, or add cooked and chopped lean beacon bits (see recipe modifications in back of book). Serve on individual salad plates. Serves 6.

FOOD EXCHANGES: Carbohydrate: 2; Protein: 0; Fat: 3
BREAD SUGGESTION: Pumpkin Surprise Bread

REAL STYLE
Presentation supplies:
- *Shallow, clear bowl*
- *Whole cranberries*
- *Oranges sliced in rounds*
- *Floating white candles, one large or three small*
- *Gold, green, or crimson napkins and placemats*

This centerpiece will complement the rich colors of the salad and bread. Place the cranberries and orange rounds in a shallow, clear bowl. Pour water into the clear bowl until it is two-thirds full, making sure the water covers the cranberries and orange rounds. Then place three floating candles and/or flowers on the surface of the water.

Place the salad ingredients and dressing into a large clear bowl, and use white dishes for a crisp look. Colored napkins folded and placed to the left of the salad fork will create a completed setting.

Green Bean Salad and New Potatoes

¼ pound small new potatoes, quartered or halved
3 ounces small, stemmed green beans
1½ teaspoons freshly ground black pepper
2 green onions, minced
2 tablespoons extra virgin olive oil
3 small ripe tomatoes, sliced in sixths
2 tablespoons fresh chopped basil
2 tablespoons balsamic vinegar
salt to taste

Cook the potatoes until tender in a large saucepan of boiling water. In a separate pot of boiling water, cook the green beans until tender, timing it so the potatoes and beans are done at the same time.

Drain and place together in one large bowl. While the potatoes and beans are still hot, add the pepper, minced green onions, and olive oil, and gently toss so that the potatoes and beans are evenly coated. The vegetables will absorb more of the onion and olive oil flavors if they are still hot.

FOOD EXCHANGES: Carbohydrate: 1.5; Protein: 0; Fat: 1
BREAD SUGGESTION: Onion Dill Bread

Immediately before serving add the tomato pieces, basil, vinegar, and salt, then gently toss one more time. This salad is best served warm, but is also good served chilled. It is a great choice for a ladies' light lunch.

Serves 4 (small servings).

REAL STYLE
Presentation supplies:
- *Three clear vases*
- *Two short, wide-mouth vases or clear glasses*
- *Fresh, long-stemmed flowers*
- *Two votive or tapered candles*
- *Dry rice or sand*
- *Lavender-colored paper plates and napkins*
- *Lavender-scented spray*

This salad can be served with a pork or beef roast. Choose lavender as the color theme for this table setting. Place three, varied, slim, clear vases filled with purple, long-stemmed flowers in the middle of table. Add two more wide-mouth, short vases for long tapers or votive candles secured with rice or sand. Use lavender-colored paper plates and napkins to complete the setting, and spray a sent of lavender in the air.

Heavenly Coleslaw

- 4 cups shredded cabbage
- 1 cup miniature marshmallows
- 1 8-ounce can pineapple chunks, drained
- ½ cup chopped celery
- 1 medium apple, cubed
- ¼ cup low-fat mayonnaise
- ¼ cup plain yogurt

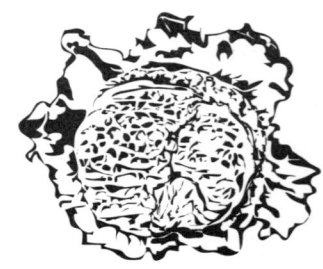

In a large bowl combine all ingredients thoroughly. Chill about 30 minutes. Before serving, toss again lightly to moisten. Serves 10.

FOOD EXCHANGES: Carbohydrate: 2; Protein: 0; Fat: 0
BREAD SUGGESTION: Diabetic Cheddar Cornbread

REAL STYLE
Presentation supplies:
- *One whole pineapple, cored, but left intact on bottom*
- *Two large red apples, cut in half horizontally*
- *Three votive candles*
- *Fresh red carnations, daises, and baby's breath*
- *White, red, or yellow napkins*

Place the cored pineapple in the center of the table and pour in a small amount of water so that it becomes a vase. Place flowers and other foliage in the pineapple vase. Cut both apples in half, sideways, and create round indentions for votive candles. Brush the apples in lemon or pineapple juice to prevent discoloration. Use only three apple halves for the votive candles. Place the candles around the pineapple centerpiece. To complete the casual look, use natural woven place mats or a casual tablecloth, and place napkins in colors that match the flowers or fruit to the left of the utensils at each setting.

Italian Pasta and Vegetable Salad

- **8 ounces uncooked Rotelle pasta**
- **3 cups assorted fresh vegetables cut into bite-sized pieces (broccoli, carrots, tomatoes, bell peppers, mushrooms, artichoke hearts, red onions, cauliflower)**
- **½ cup cubed mozzarella cheese**
- **½ cup grated parmesan cheese**

Cook pasta according to package directions. Drain well and rinse in a colander, coat lightly with oil to prevent sticking, then set aside. Choose a vinaigrette dressing from the dressings section and whisk ingredients together in a medium bowl. In a large bowl, toss the pasta together with vegetables and cheese. Add the dressing, toss, and chill before serving. Serves 6.

Variation: Omit the pasta, and add strips of salami, pepperoni, and cherry tomatoes.

FOOD EXCHANGES: Carbohydrate: 2; Protein: 0; Fat: 1
BREAD SUGGESTION: French Bread

REAL STYLE
Presentation supplies:
- *One or two fresh bunches of asparagus*
- *Red twine/raffia/ribbon*
- *Medium-size clay saucer*
- *Rubber bands*
- *Red and yellow Italian peppers*
- *Strands of ivy*

Create a colorful centerpiece of fresh vegetables with asparagus spears as the star of the show. Use a loose rubber band to hold together one or two bunches of asparagus, then hide the rubber band with a red raffia bow. Stand the asparagus in the middle of a medium clay saucer, and surround the asparagus with other raw vegetables such as red and yellow peppers. Fill in the gaps between vegetables with ivy. Be sure to choose long, flowing pieces that will extend onto the table. Make your table more appealing with bright plastic or painted pottery dishes, and bright napkins folded and tied with the same red raffia.

Layered Sunburst Salad

- 3 cups chopped iceberg lettuce
- 2 grapefruits, peeled and cut in half wheels
- 2 large red delicious apples, cored and cut in pieces, brushed with lemon juice
- 3 large bananas, sliced
- 3 tangerines, peeled, seeded, and segmented
- fresh lemon juice
- citrus peel strips for garnish
- whole pecans for garnish

Dressing

- 3 ounces low-fat cream cheese, softened
- Grated peel and juice of ½ tangerine
- ⅓ cup chopped pecans
- 2 tablespoons honey
- ¼ teaspoon cinnamon
- 1 cup low-fat sour cream

In large compote bowl, arrange the following ingredients in layers: lettuce, grapefruit slices, apples, bananas, and tangerines. Set aside.

In a separate bowl, whisk together all of the dressing ingredients, adding the sour cream last.

Before serving, add dressing to the salad and garnish with whole pecans and strips of citrus peels. Serves 4.

FOOD EXCHANGES: Carbohydrate: 4; Protein: 1; Fat: 2.5
BREAD SUGGESTION: Date Bread

During the long days of summer, people enjoy coming together to share special events in one's life. So we decided to share a few enhancements with complete entertaining ideas, including menus, invitations, and fun themes for those special occasions in the lives of your family and friends. It's all about Styling with Attitude on a Budget!

WEDDING REHEARSAL DINNER
REAL STYLE
Presentation supplies:
- *Yards of tropical, bright-colored fabric for individual round tables*
- *Solid-color tablecloths and table skirts for serving tables*
- *Assorted boxes of various sizes, clear glitter, spray adhesive*
- *Candles, tapers, and small clear glass containers for votives*
- *Fresh flowers, and foliage, palm fronds*
- *Pineapples*

Serving, Buffet, or Food Table:
Create a tropical wedding rehearsal party.

Prepare three large round tables for the food table with bread and salad being only two of the dishes served. The tables are draped in white, yellow or another solid color fabric before being placed together to form a cloverleaf. A flat large cutting board is then *placed in the center to join all three tables together. The assorted boxes are then placed in the center of the joined tables with the largest and tallest box sitting in the middle on the cutting board. Place tropical fabric over all of the boxes and push it down softly around boxes. When available, an ice carving at the tallest point where the three tables meet would be ideal, however, fruit and flowers can make a palatial showing and be more cost effective. The container for your centerpiece is a whole long watermelon with a hole cut out of one end approx. six inches round. The melon will sit vertically, held in place by a hole cut into the box underneath the fabric. The meat of the melon is then scooped out half way down to make room for the flowers and foliage. Place palm fronds in first with the tallest flowers in the center of the melon. Flowers and foliage should stand the height of the watermelon container plus half again. Place votive candles in clear glass containers among serving dishes on tropical cloth. To create a starting point for guests place napkins, dishes, and flatware on one round table with a beginning appetizer.*

Guest Tables:

Guest tables are round and covered with solid fabric and skirted. Place one small box, with a four-to-six-inch whole cut in it, in the middle of each table. Cover the box with one yard of printed tropical fabric per center with all ends tucked under about four inches. Spray pineapples with adhesive spray and sprinkle clear glitter over the entire pineapple top to bottom. Set pineapples securely in box whole, over fabric. Place sticky floral clay in the top center of pineapple leaves. Place tall white or bright colored tapers in the freezer for one hour to increase burn time, then place them in the center of pineapple. Set three to five votives in small clear glass containers approximately five to six inches from the bottom of the pineapple on the fabric. Use your collection of beach shells or buy new ones from a discount store, and place several on printed fabric. Your guest table will glow with candlelight and the love and preparation you have invested for your guests. Serve individual servings of Sunburst Salad in scooped pineapple bowls seated on bright plastic or clear glass plates with doilies.

As guests enter the room put two white leis around the neck of each guest. The white honors the Bride and Groom, and when on a budget using all one color is economical.

Envelope

Invitation

Marinated Salad

- 2 cups cauliflower florets
- 2 cups broccoli florets
- 1 thinly sliced red onion
- 2 cups tiny cherry tomatoes
- 1 cup chopped green pepper

Mix together all ingredients in a large bowl. Pour your favorite American or Italian vinaigrette dressing over the salad ingredients and toss. Cover and chill several hours before serving on dinner plates. Serves 6.

Optional serving suggestions:

Before serving, add your favorite cheese in cubes, can of tuna or chicken, bagel chips, garbanzo beans, or pepperoni. Or serve over mixed greens or over garlic toast. (Note that these will affect nutrition information, see recipe modification in back.)

FOOD EXCHANGES: Carbohydrate: 0; Protein: 0; Fat: 0
BREAD SUGGESTION: French Bread

REAL STYLE
Presentation supplies:
- *Silver heat vent pipes [cut at local hardware store]*
- *Short pillar candles*
- *Paint, flowers, beads, or ribbon for vents*
- *Butcher paper for hand-made placemats*
- *3 small, clear bud vases*
- *3 gerber daisies*
- *White doilies or coffee filters*

Think about using things to style your table that do not traditionally belong there. For a terrific and creative centerpiece, use three, small heat vent pipes as candle holders. The pipes are silver in color, crimped at the top, and just the right size for white pillar candles. To change the theme or color of your table, glue glass beads or ribbons on the vent pipes, or paint them different colors.

Place small bud vases with one gerber daisy in each among the vent pipe candle holders. For each place setting, make handmade place mats using butcher paper cut in rounds. Place large, white doilies or coffee filters on dinner plates, then serve individual portions of salad on the filters, garnishing the salad with three cherry tomato halves. Use Mason jars or other funky water glasses and red paper or cloth napkins to complete the setting.

Min-tee Melon Salad

- ¼ cup mint jelly
- 1 tablespoon lemon juice
- 2 tablespoons melon-flavored liqueur
- 5 cups of your favorite melon balls

Place the jelly and juice in a small, glass, microwavable bowl, and heat in the microwave until the jelly has melted.

Add the liqueur and set aside until the mixture has cooled.

Place the melon balls in a large mixing bowl, and pour the mixture over the melon balls, cover, and chill for several hours. Serve in a ceramic bowl with a garnish of a twisted lemon slice and mint leaves. Serves 6.

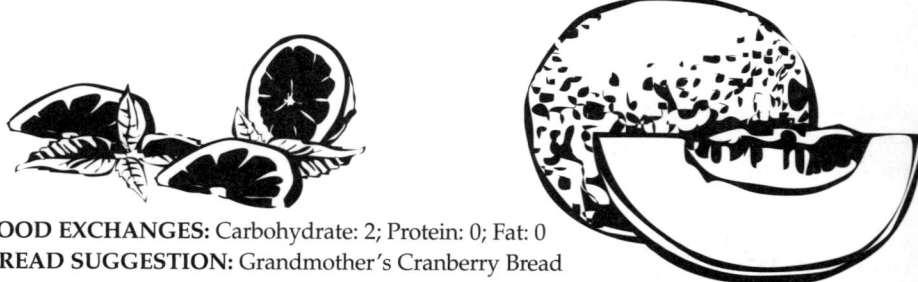

FOOD EXCHANGES: Carbohydrate: 2; Protein: 0; Fat: 0
BREAD SUGGESTION: Grandmother's Cranberry Bread

REAL STYLE
Presentation supplies:
- *Watermelon, half-scooped*
- *Fresh ivy*
- *Fresh mint*
- *Coral, green, or white napkins*
- *Shower rod rings or grape vine for napkin rings*

The centerpiece for this salad sets the mood for the dining experience. Cut a watermelon in half, length-wise, and scoop out fruit balls to be used in the salad. Save the outer portion of the melon and place it in the center of table. You will need to stabilize the bottom of the watermelon, either by shaving the bottom or placing smooth stones around the base. Fill the melon completely with ivy so that some vines rest on the table.

For the table setting, use a white paper or linen tablecloth. Place the napkins to the left of the utensils.

When serving this melon delight, place the salad in clear, Mexican glass or acrylic compote dishes. You can also serve the salad in "bowls" made from half a pineapple or cantaloupe. Place the bowls or compotes on small glass or plastic plates, and garnish each salad with a couple of mint leaves on the side.

New Potato Salad

- ¼ cup red wine vinegar
- 1 teaspoon salt
- 1 teaspoon sugar
- 2 tablespoons fresh chopped parsley
- 2 tablespoons fresh chopped chives
- 2 tablespoons fresh thyme leaves
- ⅛ teaspoon black coarsely ground pepper
- ⅓ cup olive oil or canola oil
- 1 pound small unpeeled red potatoes, cooked until tender
- 3 large celery stalks, sliced thinly
  cilantro and paprika

In a large bowl, whisk together the vinegar, salt, sugar, and herbs. Slowly whisk in the oil until all ingredients are thoroughly combined.

Gently fold in the potatoes and celery. Cover and chill one hour. Immediately before serving, top the salad with cilantro and a light sprinkle of paprika.

To make this a meal, add your favorite smoked sausages in slices. (See the recipe modifications in the back of the book if you add sausage.) Serves 8.

REAL STYLE
Presentation supplies:
- One short glass or plastic tumbler
- One medium bowl
- Hot glue
- Small plants
- Smooth, small stones
- Moss
- Green or blue paper or fabric napkins

To create a beautiful centerpiece for this salad presentation, glue a tumbler, placed upside down, onto the center of a plate. Then glue a medium-sized bowl onto the base of the tumbler. Place small plants in the bowl, and fill the gaps between the plants with moss. Place smooth, small stones around the bottom of the tumbler to complete this very natural-looking centerpiece.

Use green or blue paper napkins, or cut and fray fabric to create your own.

FOOD EXCHANGES: Carbohydrate: 3; Protein: 0; Fat: 1
BREAD SUGGESTION: Milk Biscuits

Panzanella

- 2 cucumbers, peeled, seeded, and diced
- 3 large meaty tomatoes, cubed
- 1 can large, pitted black olives
- 1 large red onion, thinly sliced
- 1 garlic clove, chopped
- 2 cups crumbled Feta cheese (or cubed mozzarella)
- 2 cups canned garbanzo beans, well drained
- 2 cups fresh basil leaves, chopped

olive oil & red wine vinegar to taste, or use the basic vinaigrette recipes for Italian at the end of the salads section

salt & pepper to taste

In a large bowl, toss together the vegetables, cheese, beans, and basil. Drizzle with olive oil, then add salt and pepper. Cover the mixture and let it sit for about one hour. Immediately before serving, add vinegar to taste, then add the bread and toss with the vegetable mixture until the bread is moist. Serves 6.

FOOD EXCHANGES: Carbohydrate: 5; Protein: 1; Fat: 3

REAL STYLE
Presentation supplies:
- *White paper, cotton, or linen napkins and tablecloth*
- *Empty olive oil bottle*
- *White or clear paper or plastic dishes*
- *Fresh flowers or greenery*
- *Old jewelry for vase and napkin rings*
- *Three to five votive candles*

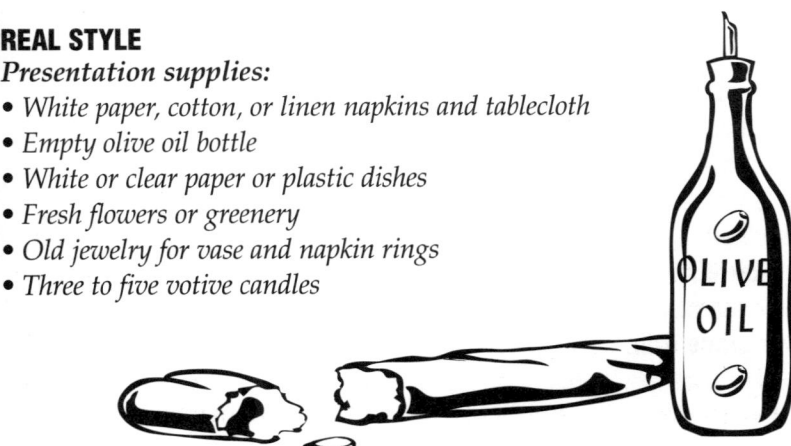

This hearty Italian salad pairs well with a broth-based soup, fish, or a baked chicken entree. Your table will be bright with the lively hues of this meal. Solid linens would provide contrast to your colorful table. Use a white tablecloth and solid white serving dishes, and use an interesting olive oil bottle as the table's centerpiece. Cut flowers and greenery, or pick some wildflowers to place in the bottle. Search your jewelry box for bracelets and/or necklaces to hang around the neck of the bottle and wrap jewelry around the napkins for a new twist on napkin rings. Set a ring of three to five votive candles around this simple centerpiece. Add some wonderful Italian music and some wine and your guests will relax and enjoy your memorable preparation of panzanella.

Peary Salad

- 1 tablespoon lemon juice
- 1 tablespoon sugar
- ½ cup low-fat mayonnaise
- 2 cups cooked cubed turkey, chicken, or ham
- 1 cup sliced celery
- ½ cup grated carrots
- 1 pound fresh pears, peeled and sliced
  chilled vinaigrette from dressings section

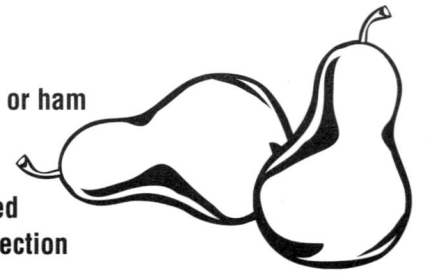

In a small bowl, mix together the lemon juice, sugar, and mayonnaise. Set aside to chill.

In a large bowl, mix together the meat, celery, grated carrots, and pears. Pour the chilled dressing over the salad, then chill the entire dish for at least two hours before serving. Serves 4.

FOOD EXCHANGES: Carbohydrate: 2; Protein: 4; Fat: 1
BREAD SUGGESTION: Quick & Easy Coffee Cake

REAL STYLE
Presentation supplies:
- *Shallow soup bowl*
- *Five to seven pears*
- *Boxwood or other greenery*
- *Gold or sage napkins*

While the salad is chilling and the bread is rising, set the table for a delightful presentation. Begin this setting with a centerpiece of pears. Stack five or seven pears in a large shallow bowl. Fill in the spaces between the pears with boxwood or other greenery. Glass or plastic bowls, china or paper plates, and paper or linen napkins can be used with equal enjoyment. Napkins in sage green, gold, or white shades will complement your table beautifully.

Shrimp Pasta Vegetable Salad

- 4 cups cooked, spiral-shaped pasta (5 cups dry pasta)
- 1 package (16 ounces) of frozen cooked shrimp, thawed, washed, and drained
- 1 cup sugar snap peas, steamed to desired tenderness
- 1 cup mini carrots, steamed to desired tenderness
- 1 cup cauliflower florets, steamed to desired tenderness
- 1 cup cherry tomatoes, halved
- 1 cup fresh chopped parsley
- 1 cup bean sprouts

In a large bowl, toss together all of the ingredients and select a vinaigrette of your choice at the end of the salads section. Serves 6.

FOOD EXCHANGES: Carbohydrate: 2; Protein: 3; Fat: 0* (*depends on dressing choice)
BREAD SUGGESTION: Quick Potato Bread

REAL STYLE
Presentation supplies:
- *Medium-size fish bowl*
- *Sea shells*
- *White sand*
- *White pillar candle*
- *Wine glasses*
- *White or natural color tablecloth*

Create a seaside centerpiece using a clear fish bowl. Pour three to four cups of sand in the bottom of the bowl and let the sand settle naturally. Place the pillar candle in the center of the bowl, and turn it slightly to set it solidly in the sand. Place shells around the candle in no particular order to create a natural look.

Use soup bowls sitting on dinner plates to dress up this salad's presentation. Garnish salad with a sprig of parsley.

Shrimp Salad

- 1 pound unpeeled, medium-size, fresh shrimp
- 3 cups of water
- ⅓ cup fat-free sour cream
- 2 teaspoons finely chopped celery
- 1 teaspoon finely chopped onion
- 2 teaspoons lemon juice
- ⅛ teaspoon salt
- ⅛ teaspoon curry powder
- 2 green lettuce leaves

Peel and de-vein the shrimp. Bring the water to a boil, add shrimp, and cook for three to five minutes or until the shrimp turns pink. Drain the shrimp well and rinse with cold water. Reserving six whole shrimp for garnish, cut each shrimp in half lengthwise, and set aside in a small bowl.

In another small bowl, combine the sour cream, celery, onion, lemon juice, salt, and curry powder, stirring well. Add the sour cream mixture to the shrimp, and toss gently. Cover and chill thoroughly.

Serve the salad on lettuce-lined plates. Serves 2 (1 cup servings).

FOOD EXCHANGES: Carbohydrate: 0; Protein: 3; Fat: 0

REAL STYLE
Presentation supplies:
- Clear, medium height candlestick
- Clear soup bowl
- Hot glue
- Small and large shells
- Three small, white, floating candles
- Sand-colored napkins

Place one cup of small shells in compote bowl, add water, and float candles. Place three large shells around the bottom of bowl on the table. Use collected shells or purchase at craft or discount stores.

Cover individual plates with curly or iceberg lettuce. Place prepared salad on bed of lettuce. Garnish with three whole shrimp on each individual salad. Provide bread and butter plates at each place setting to the left of the salad plate for crackers or bread. Use water and white wine glasses on the table to the right of the salad plate. Use the wine glass to hold each napkin until your guest has been seated. When serving wine, tie a cloth napkin around the neck of the bottle for drips. This napkin can be a different color and texture from those used on the table setting.

Simply Special Wild Rice Salad

- **1 package (6 ounces) long-grain wild rice**
- **1 6-ounce can artichoke hearts**
- **½ cup chopped green pepper**
- **½ cup chopped red onion**
- **1½ teaspoons cider vinegar**
- **¼ cup of Moore's Marinade™**
- **10 cherry tomatoes, halved**

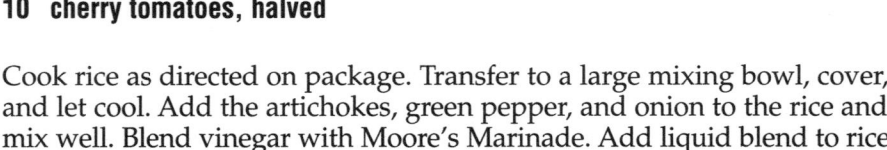

Cook rice as directed on package. Transfer to a large mixing bowl, cover, and let cool. Add the artichokes, green pepper, and onion to the rice and mix well. Blend vinegar with Moore's Marinade. Add liquid blend to rice mixture; mix well. Stir in tomatoes before serving. Serve at room temperature. Serves 4.

FOOD EXCHANGES: Carbohydrate: 3; Protein: 0; Fat: 0

REAL STYLE
Presentation supplies:
- Brown paper or butcher paper for homemade placemats
- Earthtone-colored stoneware, paper, or plastic dishes
- Rust, brown, sage, or gold-colored napkins
- Burlap to tie napkins
- Three small brown paper bags
- Three cream-colored pillar candles
- Fall or green leaves

Get wild and dress up your pork tenderloin with this rice salad. Accent your table with the earth tones of the meal by creating homemade brown- or butcher-paper placemats, and using stoneware, casual flatware, and other serving dishes with natural tones. Tie napkins with burlap or use woven napkin holders. For the table's centerpiece, fold down the tops of three brown lunch bags a half-inch several times. Stand pillar candles in each bag and tie the bags around the candles with burlap twine. Use caution when using the brown bags as candleholders—never leave them unattended with candles burning. A few colorful dried leaves scattered at their base will create a lovely, natural look. Serve bread in a deep bowl lined with brown paper or natural, woven napkins.

Spinach Berry Salad

- ⅓ cup low-fat mayonnaise
- ¼ cup orange juice
- 1 teaspoon sugar
- 1 teaspoon poppy seeds
- ½ pound fresh spinach, washed, trimmed, and torn into bite-sized pieces
- 2 cups sliced fresh strawberries (or 1 cup strawberries and 1 cup blueberries)

Combine the mayonnaise, orange juice, sugar, and poppy seeds in a small bowl. Stir well and set aside. Gently toss the spinach and strawberries in a large bowl, then arrange on individual salad plates. Drizzle one teaspoon of the poppy seed dressing over each salad. Serves 8.

FOOD EXCHANGES: Carbohydrate: 0; Protein: 0; Fat: 0
BREAD SUGGESTION: Peach Tea Bread

REAL STYLE
Presentation supplies:
- *Three clear vases, eight to ten inches tall*
- *Red food coloring*
- *Silver glitter*
- *Two white, pink, or red dripless tapered candles*
- *Hot pink, coral, or red-colored napkins*
- *Light green paper plates and bowls*

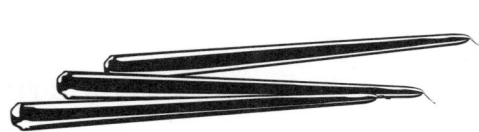

Fresh green salad with strawberries calls for a table presentation that reflects the same freshness. Fill one of the clear vases with water, then add red food coloring to dye the water a light pink color. Add silver glitter to make the water sparkle. Place the tapered candles in the other clear vases and arrange them around the water-filled vase.

Use soft green paper plates and bowls, and complement them with soft pink or hot pink napkins.

Taco Chicken Salad

- 4 skinned, boned chicken breast halves, about 4 ounces each
- 2 teaspoons salt-free Mexican seasoning
- 4 flour tortillas, 10-inch size
- cooking spray
- ½ cup chopped green pepper
- ½ cup chopped sweet red pepper
- 1 medium mango, peeled and chopped
- 1 teaspoon chopped fresh cilantro
- 2 teaspoons water
- 2 teaspoons lime juice
- 2 teaspoons vegetable oil
- 1 teaspoon granulated sugar substitute (such as Splenda)
- 6 cups shredded bibb lettuce or iceberg lettuce

Coat the chicken breasts with one teaspoon Mexican seasoning in a casserole dish, then cover and refrigerate for eight hours.

Press each tortilla into a small microwave-safe bowl; microwave at HIGH for one minute or more until crisp. These will be the taco "bowls" for the salad.

Coat a nonstick skillet with cooking spray and place over medium heat. Add chicken and cook five minutes on each side or until done. Chop the chicken into bite-sized pieces, then combine it with the peppers, mango, and cilantro. Set aside.

Combine the remaining teaspoon of Mexican seasoning with the water, lime juice, vegetable oil, and sugar substitute. Mix well, then drizzle over the chicken mixture. Arrange the shredded lettuce evenly in the tortilla bowls and top with chicken mixture. Serve with lime slices, if desired, on large plates or terracotta saucers. Serves 4.

REAL STYLE

Presentation supplies:

- *Large terracotta pot saucers for individual servings (oiled)*
- *Avocado slices*
- *Whole avocados and red, yellow, and green sweet peppers (for decoration)*
- *Serrano chilies*
- *Tortilla chips and salsa*
- *Colorful, woven placemats*
- *Medium terracotta saucer for centerpiece*
- *Paper flowers to wrap around napkins*
- *Small terracotta saucers*
- *Colorful plastic glasses*

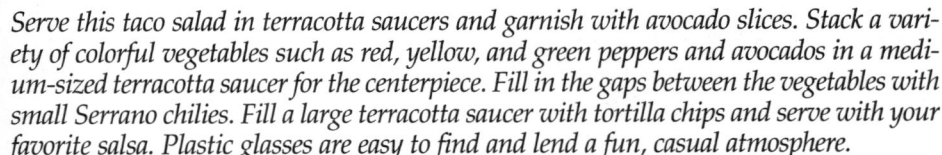

Serve this taco salad in terracotta saucers and garnish with avocado slices. Stack a variety of colorful vegetables such as red, yellow, and green peppers and avocados in a medium-sized terracotta saucer for the centerpiece. Fill in the gaps between the vegetables with small Serrano chilies. Fill a large terracotta saucer with tortilla chips and serve with your favorite salsa. Plastic glasses are easy to find and lend a fun, casual atmosphere.

FOOD EXCHANGES: Carbohydrate: 3; Protein: 3; Fat: 3
BREAD SUGGESTION: Fiesta Corn Sticks

Tenderloin Summer Salad

- 2 cups cooked, chopped pork tenderloin
- ½ cup chopped dried apricots
- ⅓ cup halved pecans
- 1 cup chopped celery
- ½ cup chopped green onion
- ½ cup canola oil
- 2 tablespoons fresh Minute Maid orange juice
- 1 clove garlic, chopped
- ¼ teaspoon black pepper
- ¼ teaspoon fresh grated ginger root

In a large bowl, toss together the pork, apricots, pecans, celery, and onion, and chill until ready to serve. In a jar, mix the oil, juice, garlic, pepper, and grated ginger. Shake to mix thoroughly, chill for an hour and pour over the salad.

Serves 4.

FOOD EXCHANGES: Carbohydrate: 0; Protein: 3.5; Fat: 0
BREAD SUGGESTION: Banana Nut Bread

REAL STYLE
Presentation supplies:
- Large platter
- Ceramic, tin, or terracotta pots
- Grass seed to grow in pots
- Raffia or ribbon
- Pastel-colored paper or cloth napkins
- Pastel-colored paper or plastic plates

This salad is an excellent choice for the lazy days of summer, and offers the wonderful flavors of apricot and ginger. As an entree it will look beautiful on a large platter garnished with additional small apricots and pecans. Keep rye grass seed handy to plant in ceramic, tin, or terracotta pots several days before company arrives. It's easy to find inexpensive small pots or tins at local discount stores, or use what you have around your house. Tie pastel-colored raffia or ribbon around the containers of grass and arrange them in the center of your table. This makes a simple and easy centerpiece sure to spark conversation.

Tuna Bean Salad

1 cup fresh green beans, steamed and cooled
½ cup sliced black olives
1 cup halved cherry tomatoes
½ cup sliced red onion
1 can light kidney beans
1 can water-packed white tuna, drained, broken in pieces
Carrot shavings

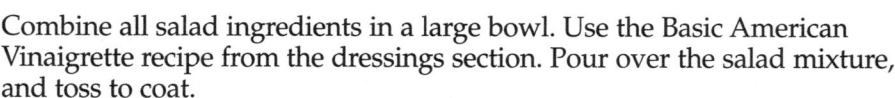

Combine all salad ingredients in a large bowl. Use the Basic American Vinaigrette recipe from the dressings section. Pour over the salad mixture, and toss to coat.

Cover and chill for one hour to blend the flavors. Garnish the salad with carrot shavings before serving in large wooden salad bowls. Serves 4.

FOOD EXCHANGES: Carbohydrate: 1; Protein: 1.5; Fat: 0
BREAD SUGGESTION: Scratch Biscuits

REAL STYLE
Presentation supplies:
- Wooden salad bowls
- Large wooden bowl or small tin tub
- Small house plants
- Moss
- Sand, tan, or sage-colored napkins

Your table can be artfully dressed with small houseplants gathered in a large wooden salad bowl or small tin tub. Get back to nature and fill the spaces between the plants with green moss. Use sand, tan, or sage-colored paper or cloth napkins for added decor. A napkin-lined basket with a simple hot bread is a treat your guests will love.

Turkey Spring Greens

- 1 cup shredded white turkey meat
- 1½ cups baby spring greens
- 1½ cups steamed chopped fresh asparagus
- 1½ cups torn bibb lettuce
- 1 cup fresh raspberries
- ¼ cup chopped walnuts

Dressing

- ¼ cup canola oil
- 2 tablespoons raspberry vinegar
- 1 tablespoon sour cream
- 3 tablespoons honey
- ½ cup prepared mustard

Add all of the dressing ingredients to a jar with a lid and shake well. Chill before serving.

In a large bowl, mix all the salad ingredients together, except for the walnuts. Pour chilled dressing over the salad, serve on a leaf of bibb lettuce on individual salad plates, and garnish with the walnuts. Serves 4.

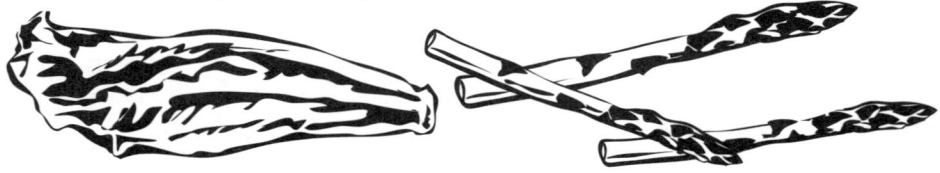

FOOD EXCHANGES: Carbohydrate: 2; Protein: 4; Fat: 2
BREAD SUGGESTION: Whole Wheat Bread

REAL STYLE
Presentation supplies:
- Red, yellow, pink, and orange Gerber daises
- Floral foam, four and a half inches in diameter, soaked in water
- Four-inch clay pot and saucer
- Three or four small rocks
- Yellow and orange paint
- Brown paper bags for homemade placemats
- Yellow paper or cloth napkins

Create a bright centerpiece for this spring salad. First paint a four-inch clay pot with yellow and orange paint. Then place a few rocks in the painted pot, leaving approximately one quarter of the pot exposed for the soaked floral foam. Pierce holes in the foam in a circle shape and place the Gerber daises in the prepared holes, creating a colorful bouquet for the centerpiece. Add water to the pot. Place the painted pot in the painted saucer. To further liven up your table, create placemats from brown paper bags and use the same orange and yellow paints to make bright polka dots on your placemats. Use yellow napkins and bright-colored plastic dishes and glasses.

Dressings

The best way to enjoy your salads is to create your favorite Basic Vinaigrette Dressing. These salad dressings are from co-author Debra Lustrea's kitchen. If you are not diabetic you'll love every ingredient; if you are diabetic, please note the food exchanges and modify the recipe of the salad dressing to fit your dietary needs. There is something for everyone's lifestyle.

American Basic Vinaigrette Dressing
- 1 garlic clove, crushed
- 1 tablespoon each dry mustard, parsley, chive
  salt & black pepper to taste
- 1 part vinegar to 2 parts oil

French
- ¼ cup tarragon vinegar
- ½ tablespoon tarragon leaves
- ½ cup canola oil

Greek
- juice of 1 lemon
- 1 tablespoon oregano
- ½ cup olive oil
- ¼ cup red wine vinegar

Italian

- ¼ cup red wine vinegar
- 1 tablespoon each basil, oregano
- ½ cup olive oil

Oriental

- ¼ cup rice vinegar
- 1 tablespoon soy sauce
- 1 tablespoon grated ginger root
- ½ cup soybean oil

Polynesian

- 1 cup orange juice
- 1 tablespoon coconut flakes
- 1 teaspoon grated orange peel
- ¼ cup peanut oil
- ⅛ cup white wine

Swiss

- ¼ cup white wine vinegar
- 1 teaspoon nutmeg
- 1 teaspoon cumin
- ½ cup sesame oil

African

- ¼ cup citrus vinegar
- 2 tablespoons honey
- ½ cup sunflower oil

Spanish

- juice of 1 lime
- 1 tablespoon chopped cilantro
- ¼ cup olive oil
- ⅛ cup rose wine

NOTE: *The recipes on these two pages make six servings.*

NOTE: *All vinaigrette dressings can be used by diabetics in moderation. See the recipe modifications section.*

If you are diabetic or simply looking for a more healthy approach to your eating habits, here are a few dressings just for you.

Buttermilk Salad Dressing

½ cup plain nonfat yogurt
1 tablespoon buttermilk powder
1 teaspoon mustard
¼ teaspoon cider vinegar
1 tablespoon light brown sugar
¼ teaspoon paprika
⅛ teaspoon hot red pepper (optional)
¼ teaspoon salt (optional)

One of the easiest ways to make this fat-free salad dressing is to measure all of the ingredients into a jar, put the lid on the jar and shake it well until mixed. Refrigerate what you don't use for up to three days.

FOOD EXCHANGES
Carbohydrate: 2.5
Protein: 0
Fat: 0

Dijon Vinaigrette Dressing

1 tablespoon Dijon mustard
½ teaspoon sea salt
½ teaspoon freshly ground black pepper
1 tablespoon red wine vinegar
3 tablespoons virgin olive oil

Combine all ingredients in a small bowl and mix with a whisk or fork.

FOOD EXCHANGES
Carbohydrate: 0
Protein: 0
Fat: 8

Honey Mustard Salad Dressing

- ⅛ cup honey
- 1 clove garlic, crushed
- 2 tablespoons stone-ground mustard
- 1 teaspoon poppy seeds
- 1 tablespoon lemon juice
- ¼ cup canola oil
- 1 tablespoon chopped fresh chives
- 1 tablespoon toasted sesame seeds

Combine all ingredients in your blender or food processor and blend until smooth. If you don't have a blender or food processor, use a wire whisk.

FOOD EXCHANGES
Carbohydrate: 3
Protein: 0
Fat: 4

NOTE: The recipes on these two pages make two servings.

A tea-time or coffee-time gathering in a garden, on a porch, or a picnic outing can be very peaceful and serene. Relaxing with tea or coffee is steeped in family traditions. So sit back, relax, and treat yourself with a friend or family member to one of these delicious bread recipes with a cup of tea or coffee; hot or cold. You'll be guaranteed an assortment of soothing moments.

Breads

Applesauce Coffee Bread

- ¼ cup plus ½ cup chopped pecans
- ½ cup firmly packed brown sugar
- ½ teaspoon plus ½ teaspoon ground cinnamon
- 2 cups all-purpose flour
- 1 teaspoon baking soda
- ½ teaspoon baking powder
- ½ teaspoon salt
- ½ teaspoon ground nutmeg
- ¼ teaspoon ground allspice
- 1 cup sugar
- 1½ cups applesauce
- ½ cup vegetable oil
- 3 tablespoons milk
- 2 large eggs

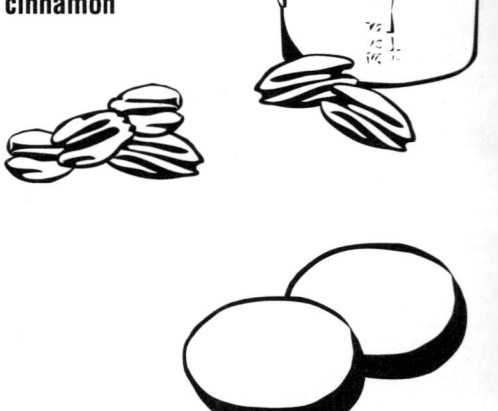

Preheat oven to 350°F. Line bottom of a 9x5x3-inch loaf pan with wax paper and grease sides. Set pan aside. In a small bowl, combine ¼ cup pecans, brown sugar and ½ teaspoon cinnamon; set aside. Sift into a medium bowl the remaining ½ teaspoon cinnamon, flour, baking soda, baking powder, salt, nutmeg and allspice. In a large bowl, mix together sugar, applesauce, oil, milk, and eggs; beat until blended with electric mixer at medium speed. Add sifted flour mixture; beat for one minute. Stir in the remaining pecans. Pour batter into greased pan and sprinkle with pecan/brown sugar mixture. Bake for 60 minutes, protecting bread with foil cover during the last 15 minutes if needed to prevent burning. Cool loaf in pan on a wire rack for about 10 minutes then turn loaf onto rack to completely cool. Serves 8.

FOOD EXCHANGES: Carbohydrate: 5; Protein: 1; Fat: 4

Banana Nut Bread

- ½ cup margarine
- 1½ cups sugar
- 2 eggs
- 4 tablespoons sour cream
- 1 cup mashed ripe bananas
- 2½ cups all-purpose flour
- 1 teaspoon baking soda
- ¼ teaspoon salt
- 1 teaspoon vanilla
- ½ cup chopped walnuts or pecans

Preheat oven to 350°F.

Lightly grease a 9x5-inch loaf pan. Cream together margarine and sugar in a medium bowl. Add the eggs and blend. Add sour cream and mashed bananas and mix well. Sift the dry ingredients together in another medium bowl, and add to the margarine/sugar mixture. Mix well. Add the vanilla and chopped nuts. Pour the batter into the prepared loaf pan, and bake 45–60 minutes, or until the middle springs to the touch or when a toothpick inserted in the center comes out clean. Serves 10.

FOOD EXCHANGES: Carbohydrate: 3; Protein: 0; Fat: 3

Banana Oatmeal Bread

- 1 cup sugar
- ½ cup soft margarine
- 2 eggs
- 1½ cups mashed ripe bananas
- 1 tablespoon lemon juice
- 2 cups all-purpose flour
- 3 teaspoons baking powder
- ½ teaspoon salt

Topping
- ¼ cup uncooked oatmeal flakes
- ¼ cup chopped pecans
- ½ teaspoon ground cinnamon
- 1 teaspoon brown sugar
- 1 teaspoon melted butter or margarine

Preheat oven to 375°F.

Combine sugar and margarine in a large bowl. Add eggs one at a time, beating after each addition. Stir in bananas and lemon juice. Sift together dry ingredients in a medium bowl, then add to the sugar/margarine mixture and blend well.

Mix topping ingredients in a third bowl, and season a greased 9x5-inch glass loaf pan with ¾ cup of the topping, which will blend into the crust while baking. Reserve ¼ cup of topping mixture for later. Pour the batter into the loaf pan and bake for 60 minutes or until a toothpick inserted in the center comes out clean. Spread the remaining topping mixture over the loaf immediately after removing it from the oven. Serves 10.

FOOD EXCHANGES: Carbohydrate: 3; Protein: 0; Fat: 2

Basic White Bread

- 1 package (2½ teaspoons) dry yeast
- ¼ cup warm water
- 1 tablespoon plus 1 tablespoon granulated sugar replacement
- 1 cup boiling water
- ¼ cup powdered non-fat milk
- 2 teaspoons salt
- 2 tablespoons solid vegetable shortening
- 6 cups all-purpose flour

Preheat oven to 350°F.

Grease two loaf pans. Combine the yeast, warm water, and one tablespoon sugar in a small bowl. Stir to blend, and set aside.

Pour the boiling water into a large bowl. Add the dry milk, salt, shortening, and remaining sugar. Stir until the shortening melts, then set aside until ingredients are lukewarm (yeast works best when mixed into warm, rather than hot, ingredients). Stir in half the flour, then beat in yeast mixture.

Gradually add the remaining flour. Turn out the dough onto a lightly floured surface and knead until smooth. Place the dough in a well-greased bowl; turn once to coat both sides. Cover and allow the dough to rise until it doubles in size.

Turn out the dough again onto a lightly floured surface. Knead gently 10 times. Form into two loaves and place in greased loaf pans. Cover and allow to rise a second time, then bake for 45 minutes or until done. Serves 32.

FOOD EXCHANGES: Carbohydrate: 1; Protein: 0; Fat: 0

Date Bread

2 teaspoons frozen orange juice concentrate	1¼ cups all-purpose flour
2 teaspoons orange zest	¾ cup whole wheat flour
¾ cup pitted, chopped dates	1 teaspoon baking soda
½ cup brown sugar	1 teaspoon baking powder
¼ cup granulated sugar	¼ teaspoon salt
1 cup plain nonfat yogurt	1 teaspoon canola oil
1 egg	1 teaspoon vanilla extract

Preheat oven to 350°F. Spray four mini-loaf pans with nonfat cooking spray. In a food processor, process the orange juice concentrate, orange zest, dates, sugars, yogurt, and egg until mixed. Add the remaining ingredients and mix until all ingredients are blended together.

Divide the bread batter evenly between the four pans. Bake about 15 to 20 minutes or until bread springs back to the touch. Cool the breads in the pans on a wire rack for 10 minutes, then remove and cool to room temperature. Serves 16.

FOOD EXCHANGES: Carbohydrate: 1; Protein: 0; Fat: 0

Diabetic Cheddar Cornbread

This recipe requires a bread machine. If you do not have a bread machine, you may add ⅔ cup grated cheddar cheese to the Fiesta Corn Sticks recipe. This will affect the Food Exchanges.

- 1¼ cups water
- 1 tablespoon honey
- 3 tablespoons butter
- ¼ cup nonfat milk powder
- 1 package (2½ teaspoons) active dry yeast
- 2½ cups unbleached all-purpose flour
- 1 cup yellow cornmeal
- 1½ teaspoons sea salt
- ⅔ cup grated cheddar cheese

Use the light-crust position on your bread maker. In the order suggested by your bread maker instructions, add all ingredients *except* the cheese. Mix on the regular bread cycle. At the end of the first kneading cycle, add the cheese. Follow general bread maker directions. Yields 1 large loaf to serve 10.

BREAD TIP: Salt is only used in bread to enhance the flavor. If salt comes directly in contact with the yeast before the yeast has had a chance to begin to work, it can hinder the action of the yeast. Keep that in mind when you are adding the ingredients to your bread machine.

FOOD EXCHANGES: Carbohydrate: 15; Protein: 3; Fat: 2

Dilly Bread

- 1 package (2½ teaspoons) dry yeast
- ¼ cup warm water
- 1 cup cream-style cottage cheese
- 1 egg
- 2 tablespoons sugar
- 1 teaspoon minced dried onion
- 1 tablespoon margarine
- 1½ tablespoons dill seed
- 2 cups all-purpose flour
- 1 tablespoon salt
- ¼ teaspoon baking soda

Preheat oven to 350°F. Grease two small loaf pans or one round casserole dish.

Dissolve the yeast in warm water in a mixing bowl. Heat the cottage cheese until it is lukewarm, then add to the dissolved yeast. Add the egg, sugar, onion, margarine, and dill seed. Add dry ingredients and mix well. Cover the dough and let it rise for 60 minutes or the dough doubles in size. Spoon the dough into the prepared loaf pans or casserole dish for 50–60 minutes or until top is brown. Brush tops of the loaves with butter or margarine before the bread has cooled. Serves 10.

FOOD EXCHANGES: Carbohydrate: 4; Protein: 0; Fat: 0

Fiesta Corn Sticks

- 1 package (2½ teaspoons) dry yeast
- 2 cups warm buttermilk (105–115 degrees)
- ½ cup shortening, melted and cooled to 105–115 degrees
- 1½ cups plain cornmeal
- 1 cup all-purpose flour
- 1½ teaspoons baking powder
- 1 teaspoon salt
- ½ teaspoon baking soda
- 1 tablespoon sugar
- 2 large eggs, lightly beaten
- ½ cup shortening, melted

Preheat oven to 450°F. Mix together yeast, buttermilk, and shortening in a small bowl and let stand five minutes. Combine all dry ingredients in a large bowl. Add yeast mixture and eggs; stir until well blended. Let mixture stand 30 minutes without stirring. Spread one teaspoon melted shortening evenly over surface of molds to grease corn stick pans. Heat pans in oven for five minutes, until oil pops. Fill each preheated mold half-full with batter. Bake for 12–15 minutes or until golden brown. Immediately remove corn sticks from molds. Serve warm. Yields two dozen, serves 12.

FOOD EXCHANGES: Carbohydrate: 2; Protein: 1; Fat: 3

French Bread

1½ cups lukewarm water
1 package (2½ teaspoons) dry yeast
1½ teaspoons salt
4 cups unbleached white flour

Preheat oven to 400°F. Place a shallow pan of hot water on the bottom rack of the oven. Grease a baking sheet and dust with cornmeal.

Place the water in a large bowl. Sprinkle the yeast over the water and stir to dissolve. Add the salt. Begin adding flour gradually until all four cups are used, thoroughly incorporating each cup of flour before adding another. The dough will be very stiff and you may need to use your hands to make sure the mixture is well combined.

Let the dough rest for 10 minutes. With a large wooden spatula, work through and knead the dough for five minutes. Do this five consecutive times, allowing the dough to rest for 10 minutes after each kneading.

Turn the dough out onto a lightly floured board and divide it in half. Form each half into a ball and let the dough rest 10 minutes more.

Roll each ball into a 12x9-inch rectangle. Starting at the long edge, roll the dough as for a jelly roll, making it as tight as possible. Seal the seam and the ends and taper the roll slightly.

Place the rolls of dough on the baking sheet, shape into loaves, and make six diagonal scores across the top of the loaf. Let the loaves rise for 1½ hours, brushing with cold water several times during the rising period. Bake the loaves 10 minutes and brush with cold water. Continue baking for 20–30 minutes more or until the loaves test done. Serves 10 per loaf.

FOOD EXCHANGES: Carbohydrate: 2.5; Protein: 0; Fat: 0

Grandmother's Cranberry Bread

- 2 cups sifted all-purpose flour
- 1 cup sugar
- 1½ teaspoons baking powder
- 1 teaspoon salt
- ½ teaspoon baking soda
- ¼ cup butter or margarine
- 1 egg, beaten
- 1 teaspoon grated orange peel
- ¾ cup orange juice
- 1½ cups light raisins
- 1½ cups fresh or frozen chopped cranberries

Preheat oven to 350°F. Grease a 9x5x3-inch loaf pan. Sift flour, sugar, baking powder, salt, and baking soda into a large bowl. Cut in the butter until the mixture is crumbly. Add the egg, orange peel, and orange juice all at once. Stir until the mixture is evenly moist. Fold in the raisins and cranberries and spoon into the loaf pan. Bake for one hour and ten minutes, or until a toothpick inserted in the center comes out clean. Remove the bread from the pan and let it cool on a wire rack. You may choose to substitute cranberries for the raisins for an all-cranberry bread! Serves 10.

FOOD EXCHANGES: Carbohydrate: 4; Protein: 0; Fat: 0

Lemon Bread

- ¾ cup butter or margarine
- 2 cups sugar
- 4 eggs
- 3 cups all-purpose flour
- 2 teaspoons baking powder
- ¼ teaspoon salt
- 1 cup milk
- 1 lemon
- 1 cup nut meats

Glaze
- 1 cup lemon juice
- ½ cup sugar
- 1 teaspoon poppy seeds

Preheat oven to 350°F. Grease three 8½x4-inch bread pans.

Cream together the butter and sugar. Add the eggs one at a time. Beat until creamy, then set aside. In a separate bowl, sift together flour, baking powder, and salt. Add this gradually to the butter mixture. Mix in the milk. Add two teaspoons of grated lemon peel, ¼ cup lemon juice, and the nut meats. Pour the batter into bread pans. Bake for one hour. While the bread is baking, mix together the lemon juice, sugar, and poppy seeds to make the glaze. Brush the glaze on the loaves after baking while they are still warm. Makes three loaves. Serves 10 per loaf.

FOOD EXCHANGES: Carbohydrate: 6; Protein: 0; Fat: 4

Milk Biscuits

- 3 cups unbleached all-purpose flour
- 1 teaspoon salt
- 1½ teaspoons baking soda
- 1 tablespoon cream of tartar
- 1 teaspoons baking powder
- ½ cup butter
- 1⅓ cups milk

Preheat oven to 400°F. Grease or line a baking sheet with parchment.

Sift together all of the dry ingredients. Cut in the butter using a fork until the mixture pulls away from the sides of the bowl. Add milk.

For quick mixing, use a food processor. Just add all of the ingredients at once and pulse until just blended. Be careful not to overprocess, because the rolls won't be as light.

Drop heaping tablespoons of batter onto the baking sheets and bake until golden brown, about 20 to 30 minutes.

FOOD EXCHANGES: Carbohydrate: 2.5; Protein: 0; Fat: 2

Onion Dill Bread

- 1 tablespoon instant minced onions
- ½ cup water
- 2 cups large curd creamed cottage cheese, warmed
- 3 tablespoons butter or margarine
- ¼ cup sugar
- 2 teaspoons salt
- ½ teaspoons baking soda
- 2 cups plus 1½ cups sifted flour
- 2 eggs
- 2 packages (5 teaspoons) active dry yeast
- 1 cup quick or old-fashioned oats, uncooked
- 2 tablespoons dill seed
- 2 tablespoons melted butter
- 2 tablespoons coarse salt

Preheat oven to 350°F. Combine the minced onions and water and set aside. In a large mixing bowl combine the cottage cheese, butter, sugar, salt, and baking soda, then add the onion mixture. Add two cups of flour, eggs, and the yeast. Beat for one minute with an electric mixer on a low setting, then for two minutes on a medium setting. By hand, stir in the oats, dill seed, and remaining flour. Cover and let rise in a warm place until it has doubled in size (about one hour).

Punch down the dough and divide in two greased, deep, 1½-quart casserole or souffle dishes. Brush the tops with melted butter. Let the dough rise uncovered in a warm place until it has doubled in size (about 45 minutes). Bake for 35 minutes. Remove the loaves from the dishes and brush the tops with melted butter and sprinkle with salt. Serves 10.

FOOD EXCHANGES: Carbohydrate: 4; Protein: 1; Fat: 2

Peach Tea Bread

- ⅓ cup plus 1½ cups sugar
- ⅓ cup plus 2 cups all-purpose flour
- 2 tablespoons plus ½ cup butter, softened
- 1 tablespoon ground cinnamon
- 1 teaspoon baking powder
- ½ teaspoon baking soda
- ½ teaspoon salt
- 1 (8 ounce) package cream cheese, softened
- 2 large eggs
- ½ cup milk
- 1 teaspoon vanilla extract
- 1 cup peach preserves

Preheat oven to 350°F. Flour and grease a 12-cup Bundt pan.

Mix together ⅓ cup sugar, ⅓ cup flour, two tablespoons butter, and cinnamon and stir with a fork until crumbly. Sprinkle mixture onto bottom of greased pan; set aside.

In a small bowl, mix together remaining flour and the next three ingredients and set aside.

Beat together cream cheese and remaining butter in a mixer at medium speed until creamy; beating well, gradually add remaining sugar. Add each egg individually, beating just until each yellow yolk is mixed in.

Add flour mixture to cream cheese/butter mixture alternating with milk; begin and end with the flour mixture. At low speed, beat until just blended after each mixture is added. Add vanilla and stir.

Pour half the batter into the greased pan; spread peach preserves over batter, leaving a ½-inch space around side and middle of pan to prevent sticking. Pour remaining batter over preserves, spreading gently with a spatula.

Bake for 60 minutes or until a toothpick comes out clean. Cool in Bundt pan on a wire rack for about 10 minutes, then turn onto rack to completely cool. Yields one, 10-inch cake. Serves 10.

FOOD EXCHANGES: Carbohydrate: 5; Protein: 0; Fat: 4

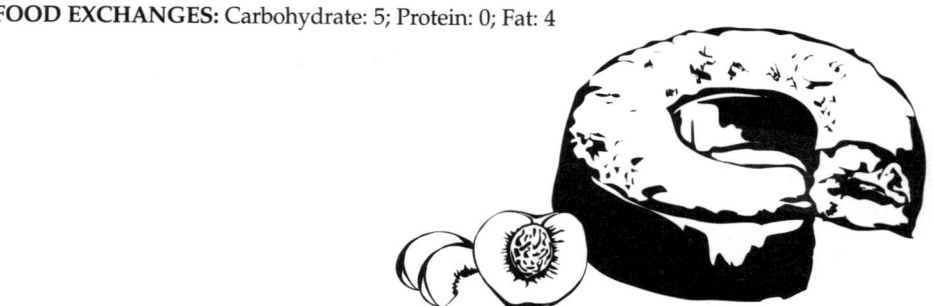

Peanut Butter Bread

- 1¾ cups all-purpose flour
- 2 teaspoons baking powder
- ½ teaspoon salt
- ¼ teaspoon baking soda
- ¾ cup creamy peanut butter
- ⅓ cup shortening
- ⅔ cup sugar
- 2 eggs, slightly beaten

Preheat oven to 350°F. Grease a 9x5x3-inch loaf pan.

Sift flour, baking powder, salt, and baking soda into a medium bowl, then set aside.

In a large bowl, beat peanut butter and shortening with an electric mixer at medium speed until the mixture is smooth, then add the sugar, beating until the mixture is creamy. Beat in eggs one at a time until blended. Stir dry ingredients into batter. Do not overmix. Spoon into the loaf pan, and bake for 50 minutes or until a toothpick inserted in the center comes out clean. Cool completely on wire rack. Makes one loaf. Serves 10.

FOOD EXCHANGES: Carbohydrate: 2.5; Protein: 0; Fat: 3.5

Pumpkin Surprise Bread

- ⅓ cup soft margarine
- 1 cup brown sugar (or applesauce)
- ½ teaspoon salt
- 1 cup canned pumpkin
- 2 eggs
- 1 teaspoon baking soda
- ½ teaspoon cinnamon
- ¼ teaspoon cloves
- 1¾ cups whole wheat flour
- ½ cup oat bran or wheat germ
- ⅓ cup milk

Preheat oven to 350°F.

In a mixing bowl, combine all of the ingredients and mix until well blended. Pour into two greased mini-loaf pans and bake 50–60 minutes. Makes two loaves. Serves 10.

FOOD EXCHANGES: Carbohydrate: 2; Protein: 0; Fat: 1

Quick and Easy Coffee Cake

- ½ cup chopped pecans
- ¼ cup sugar
- 1 tablespoon plus 1 teaspoon ground cinnamon
- 1 tablespoon butter, softened
- 2 cups all-purpose flour
- 1 tablespoon baking powder
- ½ teaspoon salt
- ½ cup sugar
- ½ cup butter
- 1 large egg, lightly beaten
- 1 cup milk
- 1 teaspoon vanilla extract

Preheat oven to 350°F. Flour and grease a 9-inch-square cake pan and set aside.

Mix the first four ingredients in a small bowl; stir with a fork until crumbly and set aside.

Mix together flour and the next three ingredients in a large bowl; fold in ½ cup butter with a pastry blender until mixture looks like coarse meal.

Mix together egg, milk, and vanilla; add to flour mixture and stir until dry ingredients are just moist. Pour batter into greased cake pan and sprinkle top with pecan mixture.

Bake for 30–35 minutes or until a toothpick comes out clean. Cool loaf in pan on a wire rack for about 10 minutes. Cut into squares and serve warm. Serves 8.

FOOD EXCHANGES: Carbohydrate: 2; Protein: 1; Fat: 3

Quick Potato Bread

- **1 loaf frozen white bread dough, thawed**
- **¼ cup dry potato flakes**
  boiling water
- **1 teaspoon salt (optional)**

Preheat oven to 350°F. Grease a loaf pan.

Pull the dough into small pieces. Dip each piece into the potato flakes, using about two-thirds of the flakes. Roll around and twist the dough to fully incorporate the flakes, then form the pieces into a single loaf.

Place the dough in the loaf pan, then using your fingers and palm of your hand, flatten the dough in the bottom of the pan. Be sure to spread to touch all sides and corners.

Brush the loaf with boiling water, then sprinkle the remaining flakes on top. Press the flakes into the dough with the back of a spoon. Salt the top as desired. Cover the loaf and set aside, allowing the dough to rise until it more than doubles in size. Bake for 30 minutes or until golden brown. Serves 10.

FOOD EXCHANGES: Carbohydrate: 1; Protein: 0; Fat: 0

Savory Orange Bread

- 1 cup orange juice
- 1 package (2½ teaspoons) dry yeast
- 2 tablespoons honey
- 1 tablespoon butter or oil
- 1 teaspoon salt
- grated rind of one orange
- 1 teaspoon grated nutmeg
- 2½ to 3 cups flour (white, whole wheat, or a mixture)
- ½ cup shredded candied orange peel (optional)

Preheat oven to 375°F. Heat orange juice until lukewarm. Sprinkle on yeast and dissolve by stirring. Add honey, butter or oil, salt, grated orange rind, nutmeg, and flour. Mix together, cover and let rise until twice the original size.

When the dough has risen, place it on a floured surface and knead in the optional peel. Let the dough rest for 5–10 minutes. Mold into a loaf and place in oiled loaf pan. Let the dough rise again until twice the original size. Bake for 40–50 minutes. Remove bread from pan immediately and cool on a wire rack. Serves 16.

FOOD EXCHANGES: Carbohydrate: 2; Protein: 0; Fat: 0

Scratch Biscuits

2 cups Refrigerator Biscuit Mix (see below)
½ cup milk

Preheat oven to 475°F. Mix together Refrigerator Biscuit Mix and milk; stir with a fork until dry ingredients are just moist. Place dough on a lightly floured surface and knead gently 10–12 times or until not sticky. Pat or roll dough out to half an inch thick and cut with a floured, two-inch biscuit cutter. Place biscuits one inch apart on a large, lightly greased cookie sheet. Bake 8–10 minutes or until golden. Yields about one dozen. Serves 6.

Refrigerator Biscuit Mix

- **8 cups all-purpose flour**
- **3 tablespoons plus 1 teaspoon baking powder**
- **2 teaspoons salt**
- **2 tablespoons sugar**
- **1½ cups shortening**

Sift together all dry ingredients in a large bowl. Fold in shortening using a pastry blender until mixture looks like coarse meal. Refrigerate flour mix in an airtight container for up to 4 weeks. Yields about 10 cups.

FOOD EXCHANGES: Carbohydrate: 4; Protein: 0; Fat: 5

Special Strawberry Bread

- ½ cup finely ground pecans
- 3 cups all-purpose flour
- 1 teaspoon salt
- 1 teaspoon baking soda
- 2 teaspoons cinnamon
- 1 cup sugar
- 1 cup oil
- 4 eggs, beaten
- 2 10-ounce packages thawed frozen strawberries

Preheat oven to 350°F. Grease two 9x5x5-inch loaf pans and sprinkle with finely ground pecans.

In a large bowl, sift together the flour, salt, baking soda, and cinnamon. Add the sugar. Make a well in the center of the dry ingredients and place the oil, eggs, and strawberries into the well. Gently mix all of the ingredients.

Pour into the prepared loaf pans and bake for 60 minutes or until straw inserted in the middle comes out clean. Serves 10.

FOOD EXCHANGES: Carbohydrate: 4; Protein: 1; Fat: 6

Spicy Cheese Straws

- **4 ounces (approximately 1¼ cups) finely grated, extra-sharp low-fat cheddar cheese**
- **½ teaspoon ground cumin**
- **¼ teaspoon cayenne, or to taste**
- **1 sheet (about ½ pound) frozen puff pastry, thawed**
  egg wash made by beating 1 large egg with 2 teaspoons of water
- **1 tablespoon cumin seed**
  coarse sea salt to taste

Preheat oven to 400°F. Grease two baking sheets. Toss together the cheese, ground cumin, and cayenne; set aside.

On a lightly floured surface, roll out the pastry into a 14x12-inch rectangle and brush with the egg wash. Cut the pastry in half crosswise, forming two 7x12-inch rectangles. Sprinkle cheese mixture over one rectangle and top with other rectangle, egg-wash side down, pressing it firmly to force out any air pockets. Gently roll out the pastry to make the layers adhere (the rectangle should be about 7½ x 12½ inches). Brush the pastry with some remaining egg wash and sprinkle evenly with cumin seeds and sea salt.

With a sharp knife cut the pastry into strips about 7½ inches long and ½ inch wide. Twist the strips and arrange on baking sheets, pressing the ends onto the sheet to keep strips twisted. Arrange cheese straws about one inch apart on baking sheets and bake for 10 to 12 minutes, or until pale golden. Serve cheese straws warm or at room temperature.

Makes about 24 cheese straws. Serves 6.

Cheese straws may be prepared and frozen before baking for up to two weeks. Freeze cheese straws on a baking sheet for one hour or until frozen, and transfer to a resealable freezer bag. Do not thaw the cheese straws before baking.

FOOD EXCHANGES: Carbohydrate: 2; Protein: 5; Fat: 6

Whole Wheat Bread

1. package (2½ teaspoons) active dry yeast
2. cups warm water
3. cups unbleached all-purpose flour or bread flour
2. tablespoons sugar
½ cup hot water
2. teaspoons salt
½ cup brown sugar
3. tablespoons shortening
3. cups whole wheat flour

Preheat oven to 350°F. Lightly grease two 9x5x5-inch loaf pans. Add the yeast to the warm water. Stir in the flour and sugar. Beat the mixture until smooth, either by hand or with a mixer. Set the mixture in a warm place to "proof" until it becomes foamy and bubbly (up to one hour). Combine the hot water, salt, brown sugar, and shortening. Stir, then allow to cool to lukewarm (yeast works best when mixed into warm, rather than hot, ingredients). Add to the bubbly flour mixture. Stir in the whole wheat flour and beat until smooth, but do not knead. Divide the dough and place in loaf pans, cover, and set in a warm place until the dough doubles in size. Bake for 50 minutes. Serves 10 per loaf.

FOOD EXCHANGES: Carbohydrate: 4; Protein: 0; Fat: 0

Helpful Hints for Baking Bread

1. No store-bought breads can fill your home with the aromas and anticipated taste of hot, fresh-out-of-the oven bread. Personal pride and satisfaction will abound from the compliments you will receive.

2. Nonstick pans with a dark surface absorb too much heat, which causes breads to overcook or burn on the bottom. Choose light-colored cookware for all baking.

3. "Folding" to combine ingredients means to use a big spoon or spatula to mix ingredients with deep, slow "folds" involving as much air as possible.

4. Salt will slow the action of yeast in bread production. It is only used to enhance flavor.

5. Great bakers are made through practice. Remember this though, "perfect" practice gives "perfect" results.

We feel that dining with family and friends doesn't have to be an elaborate meal. Whether you are celebrating a birthday, an office promotion, or having a tea party with friends, you can easily spice up these special events with style. Styling with the right attitude on a budget is all about knowing proper etiquette, having real manners, and knowing how to reinvent props that you have in your home or knowing where to go to find the proper supplies. We hope that the following do's and don'ts for dining, dressing, and responding to these special events will be beneficial for you, your family, and your friends.

Sit down, relax, and create your own style with the right attitude with . . .

Edie Hand and Darlene Real

Etiquette and Style

Place Setting

Real style begins with a properly set table . . .

Informal Place Setting

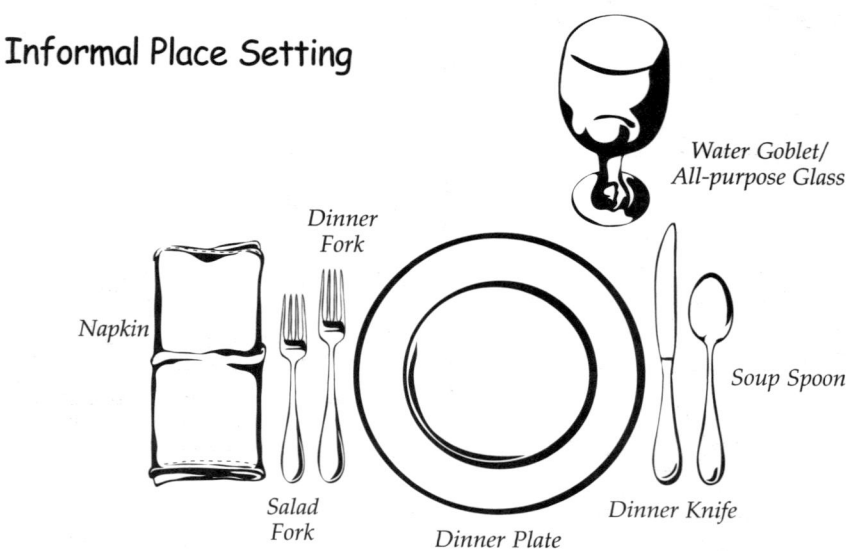

Napkins

Crown Fold

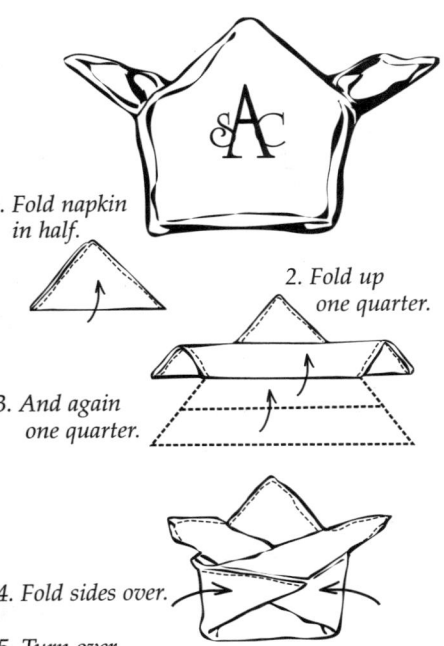

1. Fold napkin in half.
2. Fold up one quarter.
3. And again one quarter.
4. Fold sides over.
5. Turn over.

Three-Pleat Fold

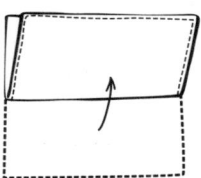
1. Fold napkin in half.

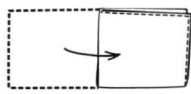
2. And in half again.

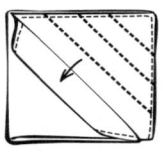
3. Fold down top flap.

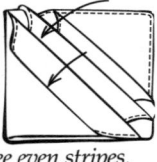
4. tuck in second and third flaps making three even stripes.

4. Turn back sides.

5. Insert card or flower.

The Basics of Dining Etiquette

Smart and Easy Etiquette Dining Tips

- Before salting or seasoning, taste your food to let the cook or chef know you believe in their cooking abilities. After tasting feel free to make slight adjustments.

- Buttering a whole roll or slice of bread is considered bad manners. Tear bread into bite-size pieces and butter one piece at a time.

- When coffee and tea are offered, its better to say "no thank you" than to turn your cup over in the saucer.

- When served soup, eat slowly and quietly from the side of your spoon. Fill your spoon by dipping the spoon forward away from you.

Smart and Easy Napkin Rules

- Napkin should be placed in your lap as soon as you are seated, in a restaurant, home, or boardroom.

- When temporarily leaving the table during a meal, place napkin to the right of your plate or on the arm or seat of your chair. Push your chair under the table upon walking away. Leave the table only if necessary.

- When completing the meal, follow your host's lead in placing your napkin to the left of your plate.

- When unfolding a large dinner napkin leave only one fold. Upon placing the napkin in your lap, the fold should face your waist.

- For a breakfast, luncheon, or brunch, small napkins can be completely unfolded and placed in your lap.

- Whether you received your folded napkin in your glass, on your plate, or to the left of your silverware, pick it up from the center. When you have finished eating, place it to the left of place setting. Do not refold.

The Etiquette of Passing Foods

- Family-style dining is passed from the left to the right. When being served by a server, food is presented on the left and removed on the right.

- When food is passed, allow the dish to be placed on the table before receiving.

- When passing the salt and pepper, they should be passed at the same time, not in the same hand, and placed on the table.

Limited Diet and Diabetic Guidelines
- Upon accepting an invitation, make your host or hostess aware of your dietary needs.

- When receiving an invitation to a restaurant, call and ask for special food accommodations, or if arrangements can be made upon your arrival.

- If you need to eat at certain intervals, be prepared for the cocktail hour and extended conversation before the meal is served.

Etiquette Tips for the Host, Hostess, and Guest
- Each guest is honoring the host and hostess by their presence. It is important to the guest to be acknowledged by the host or hostess, so greet guests warmly and verbalize how glad you are they came.

- Ask about special dietary needs for each guest.

- Plan and organize the menu in advance so you can be free to socialize.

- Make the stress of attending a special event easy on guests by seating people of like interests together.

- When planning the event menu, take into consideration the level of difficulty of the foods you choose.

The Right Attitude with Real Manners

Do's and Don'ts for Dining, Dressing & Responding

Do dress formally when attending a formal dinner.

Men: Formal wear is a Tux or dinner jacket, dark business suit, black or dark navy and tie.

Women: Formal dinner dress is long to the floor or ankle length.

Evening slacks are acceptable but not preferred, as are cocktail dresses.

Do ask your host or hostess what attire is required when a telephone invitation is extended.

Do dress to your highest standard when dining for formal, informal, and casual events. This displays respect for your host, hostess and yourself.

Do place your handbag and other personal items beside you in your chair, in your lap or at your feet, out of the path of the host, hostess, or wait staff.

Do turn off cell phones and beepers unless it is absolutely necessary for you to keep in touch with children or patients. Even then these items should be set to vibrate rather than ring.

Do respond within two to four days after receiving an invitation.

Do respond in the manner requested by the host: by post, email, or phone.

Don't take off your coat and tie when wearing a tuxedo even if the second event in the same evening is more casual.

Don't be an aroma distraction from the meal with too much aftershave or fragrance.

Don't remove shoes under the table when dining.

Don't wear noisy accessories such as earrings, bracelets, necklaces, watches, beepers, or cell phones.

Real Thank You's with the Right Attitude

Do say thank you no matter how big or small the action.

Do be timely with a thank you, the sooner the better.

Don't neglect a thank you if there is no time to send a written note. Respond verbally and follow up with a written note when time allows.

Do be specific about the deed or gift given when writing thank-you notes.

Don't be in a rush to write thank you-notes, plan time to create.

Do teach children early how and when to say and write thank you's.

Don't throw away thank-you notes that have been sent to you with beautiful passages. Save them and repeat the words of appreciation to someone who deserves a special thank you.

Know Your Ingredients

Conversion Tables

Liquid Measures

American (Standard Cup)   **Metric Equivalent**

American (Standard Cup)	Metric Equivalent
1 teaspoon = ⅙ fluid ounce	5 ml
1 tablespoon = ½ fluid ounce	15 ml
1 cup = ½ pint = 8 fluid ounces	237 ml
1 pint = 16 fluid ounces	473 ml
1 quart = 2 pints = 32 fluid ounces	946 ml

British (Standard Cup)	Metric Equivalent
1 teaspoon = ⅓ fluid ounce	6 ml
1 tablespoon = 0.55 fluid ounces	17 ml
1 cup = ½ pint = 10 fluid ounces	284 ml
1 pint = 20 fluid ounces	570 ml
1 quart = 2 pints = 40 fluid ounces	1.1 liter

1 cup = 16 tablespoons   1 tablespoon = 3 teaspoons

Solid Measures

American/British	Metric Equivalent
1 ounce	28 grams
3½ ounces	100 grams
1 pound = 16 ounces	453 grams
2.2 pounds	1000 grams = 1 kilogram

Oven Temperatures

Degrees Centigrade	Degrees Fahrenheit
Up to 105	Up to 225, cool
105–135	225–275, very slow
135–160	275–325, slow
175–190	350–375, moderate
215–230	400–450, hot
230–260	450–500, very hot
260	500, extremely hot

Recipe Modifications for Lowering Fat, Sugar, Salt, and Adding Fiber

Instead of:	Use:
1 whole egg	¼ cup egg substitute or 2 egg whites or 1 egg white plus 1 tsp oil
1 egg yolk	1 egg white
1 cup vegetable oil (can reduce by ⅓ in recipes)	1 cup olive or canola oil
1 cup butter (can reduce by ⅓ in recipes)	⅞ cup olive or canola oil or 1 cup liquid margarine or liquid Butter Buds
1 cup shortening (can reduce by ⅓ in recipes)	¾ cup olive or canola oil
½ cup shortening any oil in a baked recipe	⅓ cup olive or canola oil or same amount of moist food such as applesauce, yogurt, or prunes
1 cup whole milk	1 cup skim or nonfat buttermilk
1 cup buttermilk	1 tablespoon lemon juice or vinegar and skim milk to make 1 cup

Instead of:	**Use:**
1 cup light cream	1 cup fat-free half & half or 1 cup evaporated skin milk
1 cup sour cream or 1 cup cream cheese	1 cup fat-free sour cream or 1 cup plain, low-fat yogurt
1 cup thin white sauce	1 tablespoon oil plus 1 tablespoon flour plus 1 cup skim milk
1 cup medium white sauce	2 tablespoons oil plus 4 tablespoons flour plus 1 cup skim milk
1 cup thick white sauce	3 tablespoons oil plus 4 tablespoons flour plus 1 cup skim milk
cream soups	1 cup thin white sauce plus ¼ cup celery, 1 cup mushrooms and ⅕ chicken bouillon cube or reduced fat canned soups
1 cup white flour	1 cup minus 2 tablespoons whole wheat flour, and decrease oil in recipe by 1 tablespoon and increase liquid by 1–2 teaspoons, or use ½ cup white plus ½ cup wheat
mayonnaise	yogurt or fat free/low fat mayonnaise
sugar	Can generally be reduced by ½ in recipes

Carbohydrate Exchanges

Bread

One bread exchange equals:
15 grams carbohydrates, 3 grams protein, 0–1 gram fat and 80 calories

bagel	½ (1 ounce)
Bread, reduced-calorie	2 slices (1½ ounces)
Bread, white, whole-wheat, pumpernickel, rye	1 slice (1 ounce)
Bread sticks, crisp, 4 in. long x ½ in.	2 (⅔ ounce)
English muffin	½
Hot dog or hamburger bun	½ (1 ounce)
Pita, 6 in. across	½
Roll, plain, small	1 (1 ounce)
Raisin Bread, unfrosted	1 slice (1 ounce)
Tortilla, 6 in. across, corn or flour	1
Waffle, 4½ in. square, reduced-fat	1

Starchy Vegetables

One starchy vegetable exchange equals:
15 grams carbohydrates, 3 grams protein, 0–1 gram fat and 80 calories

Baked beans	⅓ cup
Corn	½ cup
Corn on cob, medium	1 (5 ounces)
Mixed vegetables with corn, peas, or pasta	1 cup
Peas, green	½ cup
Plantain	½ cup
Potato, baked or boiled	1 small (3 ounces)
Potato mashed	½ cup
Squash, winter (acorn, butternut, pumpkin)	1 cup
Yam (sweet potato), plain	½ cup

Nutrition Tips
1. Most starch choices are good sources of B vitamins.
2. Foods made from whole grains are good sources of fiber.
3. Beans, peas, and lentils are good source of protein and fiber.

Fruit

One fruit exchange equals:
15 grams carbohydrates and 60 calories. The weight includes skin, core seeds, and rind.

Apple, unpeeled small	1 (4 ounces)
Applesauce, unsweetened	½ cup
Apples dried	4 rings
Apricots, fresh	4 whole (5½ ounces)
Apricots, dried	8 halves
Apricots, canned	½ cup
Banana, small	1 (4 ounces)
Blackberries	¾ cup
Blueberries	¾ cup
Cantaloupe, small	⅓ melon (11 ounces) or 1 cup cubes
Cherries, sweet fresh	12 (3 ounces)
Cherries, sweet canned	½ cup
Dates	3

Figs, fresh	1½ large or 2 medium (3½ ounces)
Figs, dried	½ cup
Fruit Cocktail	½ cup
Grapefruit, large	½ (11 ounces)
Grapefruit sections, canned	¾ cup
Grapes, small	17 (3 ounces)
Honeydew melon	1 slice (10 ounces) or 1 cup cubes
Kiwi	1 (3½ ounces)
Mandarin oranges, canned	¾ cup
Mango, small	½ fruit (5½ ounces) or ½ cup
Nectarine, small	1 (5 ounces)
Orange, small	1 (6½ ounces)
Papaya	½ fruit (8 ounces) or 1 cup cubes
Peaches, canned	½ cup
Pear, large fresh	½ (4 ounces)
Pear, canned	½ cup

Pineapple, fresh	¾ cup
Pineapple, canned	½ cup
Plums, small	2 (5 ounces)
Plums, canned	½ cup
Prunes, dried	3
Raisins	2 tablespoons
Raspberries	1 cup
Strawberries	1¼ cup whole berries
Tangerines, small	2 (8 ounces)
Watermelon	1 slice (13½ ounces) or 1¼ cup cubes

Fruit Juices

Apple juice/cider	½ cup
Cranberry juice cocktail	⅓ cup
Cranberry juice cocktail, reduced-calorie	1 cup
Fruit juice blends, 100% juice	⅓ cup

Grape juice	⅓ cup
Grapefruit juice	½ cup
Orange juice	½ cup
Pineapple juice	½ cup
Prune juice	⅓ cup

Nutrition Tips

1. Fresh, frozen, and dried fruits have about 2 grams of fiber per choice. Fruit juices contain very little fiber.

2. Citrus fruits, berries, and melons are good sources of Vitamin C.

Milk

Milk and milk products are on this list. You'll find cheeses on the Meat List and cream and other dairy fats on the Fat List. Based on the amount of fat they contain, milks are divided into fat-free/low-fat, reduced-fat, and whole milk. One choice includes the following nutritional information.

	Carbohydrate (grams)	Protein (grams)	Fat (grams)	Calories
Fat-free/low-fat	12	8	0–3	90
Reduced-fat	12	8	5	120
Whole	12	8	8	150

One Milk Exchange equals: 12 grams carbohydrate and 8 grams protein

Fat-free and Low-Fat Milk (0–3 grams fat per serving)

Fat-free, ½%, or 1% milk	1 cup
Fat-free or low fat buttermilk	1 cup
Evaporated fat-free milk	½ cup
Fat-free dry milk	⅓ cup dry
Plain nonfat yogurt	¾ cup
Nonfat or low-fat fruit-flavored yogurt sweetened with aspartame or with a non-nutritive sweetener	1 cup

Reduced-Fat Milk (5 grams fat per serving)

2% milk	1 cup
Plain low-fat yogurt	¾ cup
Sweeter acidophilus milk	1 cup

Whole Milk (8 grams fat per serving)

Whole milk	1 cup
Evaporated whole milk	½ cup
Goat's milk	1 cup
Kefir	1 cup

Nutrition Tips

1. Milk and yogurt are good sources of calcium and protein.
2. The higher the fat content of milk and yogurt, the greater the amount of saturated fat and cholesterol. Choose lower-fat varieties.
3. For those who are lactose intolerant, look for lactose-reduced or lactose-free varieties of milk.

Fats

One fat exchange equals: 5 grams fat and 45 calories

Monounsaturated Fats List

Avocado, medium	⅛ (1 ounce)
Nuts	
almonds, cashews	6 nuts
mixed (50% peanuts)	6 nuts
peanuts	10 nuts
pecans	4 halves
Oil (canola, olive, peanut)	1 teaspoon
Olives — ripe (black) green, stuffed*	10 large
Peanut butter, smooth or crunchy	2 teaspoons
Sesame seeds	1 tablespoon
Tahini paste	2 teaspoons

Polyunsaturated Fats

Margarine — stick, tub, or squeeze	1 tablespoon
Lower-fat (30% to 50% vegetable oil)	1 tablespoon
Mayonnaise — regular	1 teaspoon
reduced-fat	1 tablespoon
Nuts — walnuts English	4 halves
oil (corn, safflower, soybean)	1 teaspoon
Salad dressing — regular*	1 tablespoon
reduced-fat	2 tablespoons
Miracle Whip Salad Dressing — regular	2 teaspoons
reduced-fat	1 tablespoon
Seeds — pumpkin, sunflower	1 tablespoon

* 400 mg or more sodium per exchange.

Saturated Fats

Bacon, cooked	1 slice (20 slices/pound)
Bacon, grease	1 teaspoon
Butter, stick	1 teaspoon
whipped	2 teaspoons
reduced-fat	1 tablespoon
Chitterlings, boiled	2 tablespoons (½ ounce)
Coconut sweetened, shredded	2 tablespoons
Cream half and half	2 tablespoons
Cream cheese: regular	1 tablespoon (½ ounce)
reduced-fat	2 tablespoons (1 ounce)
Shortening or lard	1 teaspoon
Sour cream — regular	2 tablespoons
reduced-fat	3 tablespoons

Nutrition Tips

1. All fats are high in calories. Limit serving sizes for good nutrition and health.

2. Nuts and seeds contain a small amount of fiber, protein, and magnesium.

3. If blood pressure is a concern, choose fats in the unsalted form to help lower sodium intake, such as unsalted peanuts.

4. When selecting regular margarine, choose those with liquid vegetable oil as the first ingredient. Soft margarines are not as saturated as stick margarines. Avoid those listing hydrogenated or partially hydrogenated fat as the first ingredient.

5. When cooking with fatback or salt pork, use a piece 1 in. x 1in. x ¼ in. if you plan to eat the fatback cooked with vegetables. Use a piece 2 in. x 1 in. x ½ in. when eating only the vegetables with the fatback removed. Saturated fat can raise blood cholesterol levels.

Nutrition Tips 1–4 courtesy workshop booklet, Heart College at HealthSouth.

Very Lean Meat, Fish, and Substitutes

One protein exchange equals:
7 grams of protein, 0–1 gram of fat, and 0 carbohydrate

Poultry — chicken or turkey (white meat, no skin) Cornish hen (no skin)	1 ounce
Fish — fresh or frozen cod, flounder, haddock, halibut, trout, tuna fresh or canned in water	1 ounce
Shellfish — clams, crab, lobster, scallops, shrimp, imitation shellfish	1 ounce
Game — duck or pheasant (no skin), venison, buffalo, ostrich	1 ounce
Cheese with 1 gram or less fat per ounce, nonfat or low-fat cottage cheese	¼ cup
Fat-free cheese	1 ounce
Other — processed sandwich meats with 1 gram or less fat per ounce, such as deli thin shaved meats, chipped beef*, turkey, ham	1 ounce
Egg whites	2

Egg substitutes, plain	¼ cup
Hot dogs with 1 gram or less fat per ounce*	1 ounce
Kidney (high in cholesterol)	1 ounce
Sausage with 1 gram or less fat per ounce	1 ounce

Nutrition Tips

1. Choose very lean and lean meats whenever possible. Items from the high-fat group are high in saturated fat, cholesterol, and calories, and can raise blood cholesterol levels.

2. Meats do not have any fiber.

3. Some processed meats, seafood, and soy products may contain carbohydrates when consumed in large amounts. Check the nutrition facts on the label to see if the amount is close to 15 grams. If so, count it as carbohydrate choice as well as a meat choice.

---

* 400 mg or more sodium per exchange.

Lean Meat

One protein exchange equals:
7 grams protein, 3 grams fat, 0 grams carbohydrate, and 55 calories

Beef — USDA select or choice grades of lean beef trimmed of fat, such as round, sirloin, and flank steak; tenderloin; roast (rib chuck rump) steak (T-bone, porterhouse, cubed); grounded round	1 ounce
Pork — lean pork, such as fresh ham, canned, cured, or boiled ham; Canadian bacon*; tenderloin center loin chop	1 ounce
Lamb — roast, chop, leg	1 ounce
Veal — lean chop, leg	1 ounce
Poultry — chicken, turkey (dark meat no skin), chicken (white meat with skin), domestic duck or goose (well-drained of fat, no skin)	1 ounce
Fish — Herring (uncreamed or smoked)	1 ounce
Oysters	6 medium
Salmon (fresh or canned), catfish	1 ounce

Sardines (canned)	2 medium
Tuna (canned in oil drained)	1 ounce
Game — Goose (no skin), rabbit	1 ounce
Cheese — 4.5%-fat cottage cheese	¼ cup
Grated Parmesan	2 tablespoons
Cheeses with 3 grams or less fat per ounce	1 ounce
Hot dogs* with 3 grams or less fat per ounce	1½ ounces
Processed sandwich meat with 3 grams or less fat per ounce, such as turkey, pastrami, or kielbasa	1 ounce
Liver, heart (high in cholesterol)	1 ounce

Count as one very lean meat and one starch exchange

Bean, peas*, lentils (cooked)	½ cup

*400 mg or more sodium per exchange.

Healthy Cooking Tips

1. Experiment with recipes. At first, use about ¾ of the fat suggested in the recipe. Next time reduce the amount of fat to half. Many recipes include more fat than is necessary. Although extra virgin olive oil has a strong taste, try it in recipes. Much of its flavor disappears when cooked, especially when cutting back on the amount of oil suggested. Light olive oils will provide the same monounsaturated fat and have a lighter flavor, if you find the extra virgin olive oil in a particular recipe objectionable.

2. Since you may lose some moisture when you reduce the amount of fat in some recipes, consider adding defatted chicken broth, skim milk, wine, fruit juice, yogurt, or applesauce when appropriate.

3. Steam or microwave vegetables or saute in broth. For flavor, toss with a few drops of olive oil, or a small amount of grated low-fat cheese.

4. When buying vegetables for your salads:
   - Choose more dark green and the brightest colored vegetables, such as; spinach, broccoli, Romaine lettuce, carrots, squash, zucchini, chilies and peppers.
   - Broccoli, Brussels sprouts, cauliflower, greens, peppers, spinach and tomatoes are good sources of vitamin C.
   - Vegetables contain 1 to 4 grams of fiber per serving.
   - Fresh and frozen vegetables have less added salt than canned vegetables.

About the Authors

Edie Hand

Edie Hand is a radio and television personality seen on the Food Network and regional and national television morning show cooking segments, and has toured for Unilever/Bestfoods on their "Good to Know Ya Tour" across the Southeast. She is co-host of the "News U Can Use" radio show with Ken Glickman, and is a member of American Women in Radio & Television, National Speakers Association, and a co-founder of the RealHand Approach "Styling with Attitude on a Budget" cooking seminars and special events. Edie is also the founder of the Edie Hand Foundation to benefit Alabama and national charities. The author and co-author of six books and mother to one son, Edie lives near Birmingham, Alabama, with her husband, Coach Mark Aldridge.

I share in the philosophy of Chuck Swindell, "Life is 10% what happens to you; 90% on how you respond to it."

Edie Hand's Right Attitude.

Darlene Real

Darlene Real is a professional speaker, author, and photography stylist, specializing in food, fashion, and furnishings. She is the founder of Appearance Matters, Inc. and co-developer of the RealHand Approach "Styling with Attitude on a Budget" cooking seminars and special events. Darlene coaches corporate and business clients to enhance their appearance through image and etiquette. She has three children and lives in Birmingham, Alabama.

Debra Lustrea

Debra Lustrea is a first-generation American businesswoman who has experienced success in many areas. She is a strong advocate for families and children with disabilities and works with communities to create programs to help meet their special needs. Debra promotes alternative dispute resolution through the company she developed with a nationally renowned negotiator and also founded Women Developing Leadership, a group of women, executives, and entrepreneurs who work with women in crisis to redevelop mind, body, and soul. In addition, Debra has an executive position at a Chicago boutique financial brokerage clearing house. She resides near Chicago, Illinois, where she shares her love of cooking with her family.